How to Become
a Highly Paid
Corporate Programmer

How to Become a Highly Paid Corporate Programmer

Paul H. Harkins

First Edition

First Printing—February 2004

© 2004 MC Press Online, LP
ISBN: 1-58347-045-X

Corporate Offices:
125 N. Woodland Trail
Lewisville, TX 75077 USA

Sales and Customer Service
P.O. Box 4300
Big Sandy, TX 75755-4300 USA
www.mcpressonline.com

MC PRESS

This book is dedicated
to my lovely sister and editor,
Deborah Harkins

Contents

Preface

This book applies to you.

If you are a corporate programmer, this book could save your professional life. If you don't read it, you may well become one of the many who have been laid off as programming work is shipped offshore. Or you may be the one downsized in your department in favor of programmers your IT director considers more innovative and productive.

Are you scared yet?

Good.

Your career is on the line.

What You Will Learn

I have mentored, or observed, programmers who became millionaires by using the principles and techniques in this book. What they do have, and what you'll need, are innate ability, intense focus, the will to succeed, and an understanding of the principles I set forth in this book.

Make no mistake: this book will show you how to become far more productive and well-compensated than you are now. You'll learn how to deal with the problems you face on the job, whether you're a programmer, an analyst, or a consultant. The book will also point out what not to do—the habits that hurt your ability to make money, earn advancement, or even to stay on the job.

You will discover, when you're at work on a project, that learning the language is only a small part of a programmer's job. This book aims to counsel you about all the other things you need to know.

Why I Wrote This Book

In my forty-some years as a corporate programmer, systems engineer, software developer, co-owner of a software development company, and consultant to many corporations, I have worked with thousands of programmers. I've paid attention to what they do well and what they do poorly. I've seen hundreds of programmers needlessly stuck on the "journeyman" level (meaning that they're average, sort-of-competent workers) when, with a just a little direction and more focus, they could double or triple their income and move up to jobs that are far more prestigious, satisfying, and well paid.

That's why I was compelled to write this book: I've often wished I had the time to help these journeymen pry themselves from their low rung on the latter. And so, with this book, I have set out to pass along some of the expertise I've acquired in writing computer solutions for hundreds of companies—plus the techniques I've borrowed from other talented programmers. I hope, too, to convey to you the pleasure I get in doing this constructive, highly paid work—and doing it well.

Tips for Trainees, Guidance for Veterans

Programming is a field of rapid job change. Its practitioners are expected to take many jobs, to move up the ladder constantly—possibly working only a year as a programmer at one place, gaining education, knowledge, wisdom, and experience, then moving quickly higher and higher at different companies. Good programmers grow quickly. This book will show you how to get the right job, acquire the right business knowledge, focus on what's going to be productive for you and the company, and clarify what your next career step should be. (If you're not planning your next career step, you're probably in big trouble.)

Specifically, I've provided advice for the following groups of programmers:

For the beginning programmer: How to approach and complete projects, establish an intelligent routine, borrow code, meet your manager's expectations, and—most crucial—how to become savvy about your company's business processes.

For the programmer with a few years of experience: How to move out of "dog work" (maintenance) and take on the challenging, high-visibility, high-risk projects that lead to recognition and promotion.

For the seasoned programmer: How to hone your skills beyond normal programming prowess with productivity tools and programming techniques. In short—how to stay at the top of your game.

For the programmer with an entrepreneurial bent: How to evaluate and then master the risks and rewards of a life as a programmer consultant, founder of a software company, or a software inventor.

Advice From the Experts

You'll find lots of stories in this book, for I've asked some of my most successful colleagues to outline their upward path. Since all of their paths involved a mixture of audacity, talent, ingenuity, and perseverance; I find their tales compelling. My friends and I consider our careers stimulating, rewarding, and actually very easy, because we selected (or fell into) a field we liked, one that was in great demand, and one for which we have not only aptitude but—just as important—the appropriate temperament. I have had the privilege of working with some genius-level programmers who carried me up on their way to the top. And I could not have flourished as a corporate programmers without a nearly unbroken string of excellent and caring programming managers.

A Coding Fix

And for those of you who need a break from all this "career stuff" and need a code fix, I direct you to my Website, *www.harkinsaudit.com*, where you'll find a challenge—the "Twelve Balls Test," a logic test often used by IT departments to evaluate applicants' ability to think clearly. Take the measure of your reasoning power by taking the test; see how long you're at it before you find the answer.

But come back to the reality of this book. It will change your career.

—Paul Harkins
December 2003

Section 1

~

Starting a Successful
Programming Career

Tips for New and
Stuck-on-a-Low-Rung Programmers

CHAPTER ONE

How Much Are You Worth?

"Right now, you're worth no more than you are currently being paid...your information technology manager has coolly evaluated your skills, your work ethic, your competitors, your actual contribution to the company's success, considered his or her budget, and then quantified all of that into a salary."

Every programmer in every environment wants a savvy answer to that question, no matter what his or her programming language, hardware platform, or level of skill. What does it take to make it to the top? What does it take to earn elite programming status—the highest title, the best compensation, the most responsibility, authority, and respect?

You *can* make it to the top. I have watched—and helped—young trainee programmers capitalize on their talents to earn major success in corporate programming or go beyond programming to become software entrepreneurs. I have worked with programmers who have been caught in the corporate cubicle with apparently no way out—or up—and watched them realize more of their potential than they thought was possible. Along the way, four or five of them became millionaires. What gave them their edge was a willingness to focus intensely, to develop a career plan, and to employ the techniques I lay out in this book.

But first, the harsh truth: Right now, you're worth no more than you are currently being paid. Maybe you'd be earning somewhat more in a larger corporation in a different city. But the fact is, your information technology manager has coolly evaluated your skills, your work ethic, your competitors, your actual contribution to the company's success, considered his or her budget, and then quantified all of that into a salary. To get much more, you'll have to prove to your manager that you are significantly more valuable to him and to the IT vice-president than the programmers in the offices surrounding yours—who are also asking for a raise or more interesting assignments.

What can you do to get better? This book offers many specific details—among them, understand your company's business processes, upgrade your coding skills, become more flexible, take on the difficult projects, get more aggressive, turn yourself into a respected programming leader, adopt a can-do attitude, focus more fiercely, and make your boss and your end users look good. And, after you've become more knowledgeable, flexible, dependable, and creative—therefore much more valuable—you may have to move to a company that pays more generously to earn what you're worth.

Nice Work—and You Can Get It

The typical trainee programmer, including those without a college education or prior work experience, starts at the compensation level of typical corporate first-line managers. (The latest median annual earnings of computer programmers, according to the federal Bureau of Labor Statistics, were $53,040.) Sometimes, staff members in a company's human resources department cannot understand just why this is so, because they cannot accurately measure and evaluate the creative skills needed by programmers: Why are programmers so valuable? This book will show you why, and indicate how you can start for even more than the salary usually offered for a particular job.

And where can all this lead? The most creative, productive, knowledgeable, ambitious, and best-compensated of all corporate programmers are programmer consultants. They have moved up from being corporate employees to becoming independent programmers, whom corporations summon to resolve a programming crisis or work on projects too complex for their in-house staff. Programmer consultants (programming contractors) have refined their skills, creativity, productivity, and reputation so they can successfully tackle the hardest and riskiest programming projects. They are like the signature chefs of the cooking world. Theirs is the corporate programming job to which ambitious programmers aspire.

Everything Is Economic

Like every manager, yours has a budget. It provides the resources he[1] needs to accomplish his primary mission, which is to complete the projects assigned to him so he looks good to his manager, that manager looks good to the next manager, and so on up the corporate line. You are simply a quite expensive part of your manager's budget. To prosper in your job, you must produce the results your manager expects.

Yes, everything is economic, if only you can see it.

> My twin brother, Peter, and I—incoming freshman at Drexel Institute of Technology (now Drexel University)—were listening to welcoming speeches in the main auditorium with the freshman class, 80 percent of whom had chosen engineering. My two most vivid recollections of the orientation were that the dean of the engineering school said, "Look at the person to the right and left of you; one of you won't make it to your sophomore year." That got my attention. My brother was to the left of me, and the dean was right about the other guy.
>
> We waited for the next speaker, anticipating a thermodynamics professor, a physics professor, or at least a statistics professor. (Drexel didn't have a single computer then; we all had slide rules strapped to our belts.) Instead, out strolled Dr. Davidson, strumming on his guitar and singing that "everything is economic." We almost laughed at this "business geek." But a mere five years later, when we interviewed for corporate jobs, we realized that Dr. Davidson had it all correct, and in perspective. All our years of intensive college classes were light weapons against the power of the business economics that determined whether there was a good job; the compensation level of

---

1   Many times in this book I use "he" to refer to a programmer or a manager—not because I am implying that every programmer or manager is male, but because the sentence construction makes it awkward to say "he or she."

*that job; and how much competition there was for that job when we fi-
nally graduated.*

Even in your first programming job you should be aware of the
economic realities of corporate compensation; you need to develop a
strategy for moving quickly up the corporate compensation ladder. Programmers who focus on advancement are uniquely well positioned in
the corporation to move very rapidly up that ladder because of programming's potential dramatic impact on the company's profit and loss.

Programmers can produce significant productivity increases in virtually every aspect of their company. They often save it hundreds of
thousands of dollars with a new computerized application—but occa-
sionally they cost the company a similar amount by doing less than perfect work. Top management, stockholders, and sometimes the press
quickly become aware of the direct effect programmers have on the company's bottom line; that's why programmers are so well compensated.

You've Got to Know the Territory

There are many ways you can grow in your job. But the very first
thing you should do to improve your chances for job advancement is to
study your company's business processes.

I've been observing corporate programmers in action for more than
forty years. I've worked in billion-dollar companies in which I knew
virtually every corporate computer application the company used. I
call that overview the "comprehensive," or "single person's," view of a
company, and I consider acquiring this overview vital to the success of
every programmer. Most of the people profiled in this book have acquired this "comprehensive view"—they understand every computerized job in their company, and how it relates to the company business
processes. To be a super-programmer you should learn so much about
how businesses operate that you can acquire a comprehensive view of
a corporation with hundreds or thousands of computer users. You
can—over time, with focus and curiosity—understand virtually every
important computer application, even in a large company. That broad
picture of the company will give you a perspective that is invaluable to

corporate management, whose jobs are becoming more and more dependent on computer-related information.

Unfortunately, as most of the experts I have interviewed for this book point out, it is rare to find programmers these days who have an adequate knowledge of how business works (or, indeed, who even believe they need to acquire that knowledge).

> *Gene Bonett is founder and president of Xperia, a software development and consulting firm in Allentown, Pennsylvania. As a first-generation corporate programmer, Gene has seen it all. "I spent about three months in Vietnam," he says. "When I got out of the Marines at age 24 I didn't have a clue as to what I wanted to do with my life." Then he discovered information technology and programming—and worked his way up from computer operator to owner of a software firm that employs 42 people.*
>
> *So Gene has more than thirty years' worth of perspective. "I've been appalled," he booms, "that I've been unable to find anyone in the IT department at any of my fifty-five client companies who has the ability to take a customer order—whether it has been sent electronically or taken over the phone—and walk that order through every aspect of that business until the product is shipped and the invoice hits the accounts-receivable system. I have not found one yet. But thirty years ago, programmers in IT departments would have been able to do that."*

That is true: Thirty years ago, when the IBM/360 (an early computer mainframe) was just starting in most companies, the people in every IT department would accompany the systems analyst to the various departments that were being automated. The IT people and the analysts would observe the work of those who were performing the business functions and learn from them about the steps they were taking to do their work. We did all that systems design for the first time, taking all the department paperwork and translating it into computerized applications.

Now, three decades later, virtually all of the basic business applications have been computerized. What's now being done is perhaps more sophisticated, but the programmers work only with little pieces of the application. Programmers focus now on what's already running in the IT department, so they don't have to go out to the users and learn new things. Consequently, they do not really understand each particular aspect of the business.

> *"The problem with that is that the needs of businesses change every day," Gene points out. "So programmers have to understand business applications to make changes correctly. The department stores are forcing things on apparel manufacturing that were never done before, including extensive quality and compliance issues.*
>
> *"I find that in IT departments there is a lack of understanding of IT's role in the company, as well as what the company is trying to do and what information it needs to accomplish its mission.*
>
> *"IT departments are often narrowly focused on technology. They play in the technical sandbox. Decisions are made that don't adequately support the company's business requirements.*
>
> *"If you are a skilled IT person who doesn't routinely go out and interface with users in every department, as programmers did thirty years ago, how can you learn business applications?*
>
> *"That's where individualism comes in. The individual takes the initiative to go out and sit with someone in a department and say, 'What do you do, and how do you do it?' That door is still not closed to the people in the IT department. Programmers do have the opportunity to move in and out of these departments, at least in a small company, at will."*

Not only Gene, but other experts I've interviewed for this book suggest that programmers take courses in accounting and economics at night, in the continuing education department of your local college. At the very least, you should get an accounting package for your PC (like Quicken or One Write Plus) and do all your personal accounting on that.

Corporations do these things on a bigger scale, utilizing the same techniques, keeping track of the corporate "Ins" (with ADD) and "Outs" (with SUBTRACT), with the occasional MULTIPLY and DIVIDE thrown in. This simplicity applies across every corporate business function.

But you've got to be familiar with the flow of work, and how things are done at every stage.

Corporate programmers have the power and the position to think creatively about solutions that could be very valuable for their companies, and then to implement them. Just ask yourself, "Where is my company spending a lot of dollars?" and "What do I see that frustrates me and hinders me and others the most, and wastes our time?" Those have been key productivity questions for many years, and you are uniquely qualified—and in a position—to correct them, particularly if you get out of your IT office and visit the remote locations of your company. That is where the business functions critical to your company are taking place.

From Cutter to Coder, on Pure Grit

The profiles in this book trace the routes that ordinary people (some of them quite unlikely candidates) followed to become successful corporate programmers. Some of them took their first programming jobs out of desperation; some got ahead by simply having the courage to take action.

> As a young IBM systems engineer, I was helping a company convert from an IBM 1440 computer to the newly announced IBM System/360 mainframe. The company still had both computers in the conversion process, as the programming languages and the data formats of the two computers were different. I was teaching the DP manager and chief programmer, Gene Fluehr, the new programming languages we would be using—IBM Assembler language and a new, "hot" programming language called RPG (Report Program Generator). He would need to learn these to replace his IBM 1440 Autocoder programming language skills.
>
> One day Gene and I heard a knock on the computer room door. It was Sid Manas, who was a cutter in the cutting room, where stacks of fabric were cut into the patterns of parts of clothing with electric saws. Sid had been a cutter for sixteen years, even though he was afraid of cutting off his fingers with the saw. He timidly asked us a question: "Is programming hard?" Gene and I both answered no, we thought not. Sid then asked the key question: "Will you teach me to program at

night?" Gene and I looked at each other and said yes, since we were working nights anyway.

We taught Sid the "hot" RPG programming language, and without a single day of formal programming education—or a college education—Sid soon got a corporate programming job at another company, with the help of our references.

Sid took over programming responsibility for an incentive payroll application where tens of thousands of incentive payroll "coupons" were processed against operation rate masters to compute the sewing machine operators' pay. The payroll was run every Wednesday, to be paid on Friday, and it took about seven computer hours for processing on the very expensive corporate computer. That left little time for problems or recovery, or processing other key corporate applications. Sid looked at the key long-running program and quickly found a way to rewrite it so that it ran in twelve minutes instead of seven hours.

Sid had looked at the payroll programs with a new and creative perspective that none of the programmers who preceded him in developing and supporting that key application had employed. The company CFO who was in charge of IT gave Sid a raise on the spot, because he had solved a critical scheduling and recovery-time problem.

Sid became a successful programmer because he could draw on the particular qualities that are essential for high achievement in this field—the courage to try something new, the willingness to drive hard toward a goal, the kind of intelligence that spots a solution that no one else has spotted, the refusal to say "it's not my job."

And he still has all of his fingers.

If he can do it, so can you.

$$ The Bottom Line $$

To be worth more to your company, you've got to grow in your job. Unfortunately, the savvy that's most crucial to programming advancement is just the kind of savvy that many programmers are clueless about. What you must have to succeed as a programmer is a comprehensive overview of your company's business processes—meaning a thorough understanding of how your company's employees do each job, from purchasing to accounts payable to accounts receivable to all the various manufacturing (or other) processes to the final step in the system, whether it's customer checkout or an ATM receipt or the company's warehouse distribution system. Without this knowledge, you won't go far, not matter how brilliantly you code.

CHAPTER TWO

A Primer for Fledgling Programmers

"Paying your dues" has always been, quite appropriately, the new-comer's lot. My advice to fledglings, therefore, is to do cheerfully, with good grace, whatever work your manager assigns you.

This chapter aims to guide newly minted programmers past common quagmires and toward the sort of work most likely to lead to a high salary and respectful attention in the job market

"Paying your dues" has always been, quite appropriately, the new-comer's lot. My advice to fledglings, therefore, is to do cheerfully, with good grace, whatever work your manager assigns you. After you have spent a reasonable period of time—a year, maybe two—performing those tasks, it will be your turn to move up to the kind of work that provides the financial and psychological rewards that you're looking for. You have a lot to learn—primarily, how to approach and complete projects—before you are of much value to your company. Happily, you'll be paid well as you're learning.

When I got my first permanent job—with IBM in 1962—I found every application I got assigned was an opportunity to enhance my knowledge of interrelated business processes. And I wasn't even writing programs; I was wiring unit-record control panels. But I was going out to dozens of companies, large and small, to implement the automation of most of the business processes that were then being automated. I got to do it far away from IBM management, which was often 60 miles from any branch office. I was a de facto project manager as well as the resident IBM representative at companies installing IBM equipment for the first time, with the title of systems engineer trainee, because I was the only IBMer there.

My admonition to do your work cheerfully extends to maintenance, the "dog work" that even raw programmers sometimes consider beneath their capabilities. It is your obligation to do, amiably, whatever work you are assigned.

And maintenance does have its rewards: This kind of low-visibility programming will give you, the newcomer, time to understand what a corporate programmer does and how to do it successfully. And while you're going about your routine tasks, you'll probably be able to find an hour a day to expand your knowledge and expertise in areas outside your immediate responsibilities. That means "getting to know the territory"—acquiring an understanding of the business processes that your work is supporting.

And be advised: Maintenance may be dull, but it's not exactly safe—because working maintenance is working live. The program you're maintaining or enhancing might be moving thousands of cartons around in warehouses, or spitting money out of ATM machines, all across America. Any glitch you introduce can cause those machines to spit out the wrong bills, or stop those cartons in their tracks. So you'd better do this "dog work" well.

Here are my E-A-R-Ns for fledglings—the basics that I consider essential to any primer for programmers.

Establish an Intelligent Routine

Prioritize your projects: At the end of every day I take ten minutes to summarize what I've accomplished that day and to think through, and note down, what I want to accomplish the next day. I also review any programming problem that I have not completed or resolved that day.

Then, first thing in the morning, I reinforce that plan by prioritizing my projects. If you do all of this, at the end of the day you'll get a real feel about whether you've accomplished everything you planned and whether you can increase your workload and productivity. If you haven't done as much as you expected to, you'll realize why. Then, before you go home, you can set in place a plan that will make you more productive. The reason this is so important in programming is that these reviews prompt you to think of solutions to unsolved problems during the evening, and even during the drive to work, when your mind is at its freshest.

Critique your performance every day: How intensely you focus and how intelligently you code make an enormous difference to your employer. One thing you should certainly do to jump-start your productivity is to evaluate your performance every day (you can be sure your project manager is doing so). Every single day, as you finish a project or return from a client's office, you should ask yourself, "How productive was I today? How could I have done the job better?"

Whenever I see another programmer, senior or junior, using a technique new to me, I try to learn it. I've been doing this for forty years—because I realize that my way is not always the right way.

You, too, should look around to see what you can learn. Every day I try to reserve at least an hour of my billable time to learn something new, to use new techniques, new applications. I burn them into my brain so that I'll be able to recall them. I consciously absorb programming techniques (I'm not talking about confidential information) so that I can utilize them either by looking for similar information in the current client work or by referencing some techniques I've used before. That's something you absolutely must do to grow as a programmer, and it's how your employer gets even more productivity from you.

Check in with every member of your team or group every day: Because I work at various clients' offices in my role as a programming consultant, I also make it a point to spend a minute every day with the programming manager, reviewing my planned activities for the day. I also provide a one-page weekly activity summary for each client. This serves as the basis of a brief weekly management review meeting.

Keep your project paperwork in order and up to date and your office spotless: I know that this is the era of casual dress and offices that reflect their workers' personality. But I maintain that sloppy and disorganized project paperwork and reporting, and sloppy and disorganized offices, correlate directly with sloppy and disorganized programming. That may seem simplistic, but that's what I've observed in nearly four decades in the field. Once you've gotten into the habit of being organized about your paperwork and office, I think you'll agree with me.

I believe that all programmers, including trainees, should do all these things from their first week on their first programming job. My daily and weekly planning and my "touch base with my manager regularly" policy motivate me to complete more and more work. You'll probably find an intelligent routine just as helpful a work-accelerator as I do. (Your project summary reports have another virtue. One of the worst things you can do, when you're on a project that requires many months' work, is to have your manager say to you in July, "What was it you did the whole month of May"? and to find you can't remember doing anything of value. A project summary report in your computer can bring it all back to you—and your manager.)

Ask to Work on Major Corporate Business

As soon as you feel that you are a competent programmer in your assigned business process, you should look around you and select a more challenging and/or interesting one. Your daily hour spent enhancing your knowledge of the company's computerized business processes, and your interaction with your programming peers, should point the way to a potential next job in your IT group.

It doesn't matter why you move on. You may want to work with the programmers or the programming manager in another area, or you may want to learn the details of another business function. You may simply be bored with the work you're doing. It matters only that you do move on in order to challenge yourself.

It helps, when you're asking for a move to another area or team, to have long prepared your manager, and your proposed manager, for the request. All programming managers will give you cues about how they feel about you, especially if you drop a few hints about your interest in what they and their team are doing. That preparation may even start with your initial job interview, when you have the opportunity to communicate your goals. You are no doubt being hired to fill an immediate need, not with the expectation that you will spend your entire career in that same job. If that is the expectation, then both you and your manager are in severe trouble from the beginning, because your manager will not, by definition, have an education or advancement promotion plan for you.

Reach for the Business Function That Makes You Most Valuable

After you know several of the corporate business processes (like accounting or product distribution) and how they relate, and you are a respected and confident programmer in your company, you should move on to a plum job. Your manager probably will consider such a request, because you are a proven and productive programmer for him or her, and your request is a signal (or it should be) that you want to move on up. Ignoring your request is opening the door for your exit and the loss of a valuable programmer.

By now your manager is well aware of your strategy of moving on up, then probably out, but it is still to his advantage, and particularly his manager's advantage, to keep you from leaving and to find a way to accommodate your request. It helps if you have shown your prospective manager your understanding of the business function to which you plan to move. For instance, if you want to move from working on accounting applications to warehouse distribution, you should let your prospective manager know that you know—or are interested in learning—the flow of the company's warehouse distribution system.

Having decided what business process you want to concentrate on next, focus your one hour a day of learning on that process. The basics of the operations and flow of any major business process—accounting, manufacturing, whatever—can, I believe, be learned in two weeks of one-hour-a-day attention by an interested and inquisitive corporate programmer.

Working on mainstream corporate programming jobs is what brings you the highest level of compensation and gives you the most independence, security, and marketability. It would be wonderful if these mainstream jobs were also the jobs that are the most challenging, creative, and fun—but that won't necessarily be the case.

Almost all corporate programming jobs revolve around expertise or experience in a major business process: financial, warehouse and distribution, manufacturing, or CRM (Customer Relationship Management). You need to find the corporate programming work that is most in demand—a need for your experience and skill in hundreds or thousands of other companies. That usually means a vendor-supplied software application package with a very large installed base, a package that is so comprehensive (a.k.a. complex) that it's hard to find programmers to work on it.

Another possible consideration in your selection of the target business process, and even the vendor application package, is the location of potential companies that might hire you. For instance, expertise in comprehensive and widely installed financial software packages is probably the most universally transferrable programmer expertise, probably portable to almost anywhere in the world. But expertise in a manufacturing software package may severely restrict the locations where you can work. Now is the time to think about where you might ultimately want to live, and start planning for it by becoming universally valuable.

Note That Good Things Come in Big Packages

I've listed what I think are the best corporate business applications in which to become expert. You are likely to get the highest compensation in a company that is using (or getting) a premier, comprehensive, and widely installed vendor-supplied application software package and must keep it current. Look for a package that demands highly paid programmers to install or support it.

The estimates on the next page of the packages' relative value to the programmer's job fortunes are my own; I've based my estimates on the rates paid to independent programmers for working on these various packages. You can check my estimates by reviewing the vast numbers of programming jobs posted on the Internet.

Packages worth working on (best first):

- Financial vendor-supplied software packages. Financial software is probably the software that is most universally installed. Because of this software's importance in financial reporting, working with these packages is probably the highest-paying corporate programming job. This big-bucks job expertise should be your ultimate target, particularly if you like accounting (at least a bit).

- Warehouse and distribution vendor-supplied software packages. This software is probably the next most universally installed, and, because of its importance in the complete supply chain from manufacturer to consumer, is probably the next most highly compensated corporate programming job. If you like technical and physical applications, working on these packages should be your ultimate target.

- Customer Relationship Management (CRM) vendor-supplied software packages. These are next in terms of frequency of installation. While compensation for working on these packages varies by business, these are probably the next-best-paying programming job. If you like more customer-related and business-flow applications, aim for CRM.

- Manufacturing vendor-supplied software packages. These packages are probably installed less often than those above, because manufacturing companies tend to have more varied manufacturing processes, and tend to be larger than other kinds of companies. Still, your knowledge of manufacturing software packages can be big- bucks job expertise if you stick to the vendor-supplied function and do not get involved in the unique company enhancements and modifications to the supplied software.

- Above all, avoid unique applications!

I strongly recommend that after your first two company programming application assignments, or after several years at most, you avoid working on programming applications that are unique to your company. When your job goes, as it eventually will, you will have a hard time finding another one; your expertise in dealing with an application unique to one company will have little value in the job market.

$$ The Bottom Line $$

A willingness to do, amiably, whatever your manager assigns you to do is a crucial credential for a beginning programmer. After you have paid your dues for while—a year or two, perhaps—you must reach higher and ask for more challenging work. Reducing your risks by sticking to maintenance projects will keep you unnoticed and probably under-appreciated by upper management. The smart programmer pushes for more complex projects and chooses to work on applications that are transferrable from company to company.

CHAPTER THREE

What Your Boss Really Wants from You

Your job as a programmer is to keep your boss prosperous and happy—particularly with you.

Your boss wants to get promoted. At the very least, he wants to be prosperous, happy, and well liked in his current management position as he searches for the next step up or out.

Your job as a programmer is to keep him prosperous and happy—particularly with you. Your work can have a decided impact on his career: Your programming skill could help get him an impressive promotion, your ineptitude could cause him to crash and burn.

To your first working meeting with your programming manager you should bring a creative mind (your coding ability and experience are givens) and the energy to apply that creativity with consistent zeal. That's all you need.

Well, almost all you need. You also need—but probably don't have—an understanding of what your manager expects of you and how he will measure your performance.

Here's what your boss wants from you.

Fair Warning About Problems

Managers hate surprises. Your manager has made delivery commitments and cannot afford to be surprised with the news that your project will be late. I consider it important to spend one minute a day informing my manager where I stand with my projects—whether he initiates the conversation or I do. Then, once a week, I prepare a one-page summary of where I stand and ask him for a five-minute review and evaluation of the projects. In this interview I can ask him for another, more challenging, project.

IT management is so averse to disagreeable surprises that it has adopted effective, if sometimes low-tech, ways of avoiding them. Every change to an existing computerized application, every implementation of a new application, depends on the programmers' getting every line of code and every testing scenario correct. However, IT management cannot guarantee the success of any new application, or even any change to an existing production application, because programming is experimental. So changes can have profoundly negative consequences that are visible to the corporate office, yet the changes must be made, and new programmed applications must be implemented.

One very practical way some IT management avoids disagreeable programming surprises (and the inevitable corporate management re-action) is by refusing to allow programming changes to be implemented in production during the week of the monthly financial closing (or for two weeks before the end of a fiscal quarter). Part of the reason for this low-tech but effective solution is that many years of production have shown that there is simply little time for solid recovery procedures that redeem major problems in month-end closings, which are typically processed on weekends. The IT management on call to cover the weekend monthly closings typically cannot find and correct the programming problems themselves, and the savvy programmer is surf fishing, sans beeper.

Understanding how unwelcome surprises are to management should make you careful not to hide your dawning knowledge that your work is going to take longer than you had expected—or any other problems your manager deserves to know about.

Confidence

Managers want to see confidence and a "can-do" attitude. Many of the managers I interviewed for this book expressed irritation at programmers who react to assignments with remarks about how difficult and complex the work will be.

Almost any business process can be programmed, and that is what employers want to hear. Do not tell a client or user how hard or complicated a job is going to be. What employers want from their programmers is a can-do attitude and professional, productive results. And no geek-speak; when programmers flaunt their technical ability, managers are put off.

Positive Feedback about You

Managers want you to help them look good. You may not realize how delicate your boss's position is. He or she dreads a negative call from senior management.

The trigger for that possible call is sloppy, incorrect work or continual rework because you don't get it right the first time. Even something as simple as your show of discourtesy to an end user or someone else can stir up enough outrage to provoke such a call.

Accuracy

Coding skill alone is not enough to merit keeping a job as a corporate programmer. Your manager expects you to do every phase of your work correctly, without micromanagement from him—to be productive without prodding, and to be zealous about accuracy.

Isn't is obvious that a programmer must care about accuracy? In fact, no. I was a programming consultant to a major corporation doing a Y2K (Year 2000) conversion of hundreds of production programs to a new version of a critical software package. The package contained hundreds of programs and millions of lines of source code that had been maintained and enhanced for some fifteen years at the company before the mandated change to the entire system.

A conversion programming project team of about eight outside programmers (contractors) was assembled to implement this change. As a company visitor, I had to share a cubicle with another contractor programmer. We had little project orientation, so we plunged ahead and started dozens of programs to upgrade the application to the new level.

After I changed each program and compiled it, I tested the program against the company database of information to see if my changes and the new software worked properly, as is normal programming procedure. My cubicle mate changed and compiled his programs, but he did not test them at all to see if they actually worked, and the project manager, who had the cube next to ours, did not review our work.

Just before our first project implementation integration test, the project manager received a phone call from the consulting company inquiring about my cubicle mate's performance. "Couldn't be better," was the project manager's warm reply. Soon after that came the first project integration tests where all the project programs were run against the company data. My cubicle mate soon disappeared, and the project manager started closely checking the work of every programmer on his team.

Putting Your Work Ahead of Your Ego

Many years ago I met a top programming consultant who had a curious title—"The Shadow"—embossed on his business card. I was puzzled. Why would a competent, high-level consultant hand out cards bearing a jocular handle like that?

Having watched successful corporate programmers at work over the years, I think I have figured out why. All of the really talented programmers I've met—programmers who have developed advanced and important applications—are "Shadows." They are known by their product, not by their personality or appearance. They are compulsive about doing focused, reliable, and consistent work, with well-executed testing and documentation. And so, when such a programmer goes on to another project, no one will need to know his name, for no one will need to summon him to provide an explanation or to untangle a glitch he's created. If that happens, a programmer is not the professional that his manager wants him to be.

Some programming efforts are so massive in size and scope that they require the combined efforts of dozens of programmers. Your company wants the product of its programmers to be consistent, seamless, and attributable to the entire programming team, rather than to individual programmers, even though each line of source code was written by a single programmer who was focused on a tiny block of work. You should be ready to give the code that seamless look and feel.

The Prudent "I Don't Know"

You should always be so well prepared that you don't fall into the trap of asking inappropriate questions that can uncover your lack of preparation and annoy your manager. On the other hand, lack of grit is what keeps many programmers from asking questions that are entirely appropriate—in fact, called for.

> *Joe Cohill, Director of Business Analysis at a large apparel manufacturing company near Philadelphia, lacks patience for programmers' reluctance to speak up when there's something they don't understand. His mantra is, "Question everything. People tend to do things the way they've always done them—because they don't ask questions. I have been in meetings where all the programmers were nodding as if they understood, and then someone asked a question, and it turned out that nobody understood—they'd been pretending.*
>
> *"Assume nothing. Ask questions when there's something you don't understand. When you speak up, you verify your understanding of the task and avoid costly blunders. And that's good for your career."*

Respect

No manager should have to deal with disrespectful and uncooperative subordinates. You are being paid well to be a positive, contributing member of a programming team under the direction of IT management. Your manager may not have the technical programming skills that you have, but he does have a perspective and an understanding of corporate objectives that you do not share.

Loyalty, trust, and respect between manager and programmer are essential to the success of both members of the team. Do not belittle your manager: He is your boss because he has skills that you do not yet have. You can become much more valuable by observing and working well with a good manager. It's his job to help you with your technical issues, your projects, and your education plan. What's less obvious is that he can model for you the way to deal effectively with management.

Clearly, your boss should not ask you to do anything illegal, unethical, or outside the corporate business-conduct guidelines; and, just as clearly, you should not violate those standards either.

If you draw a bad boss, mockery and insubordination from you will only add to his hostility toward you. Programmers who are disloyal to, or show no respect for, their managers are usually unhappy and unproductive, traits that are likely to dislodge them from their position—sooner rather than later.

Your manager will probably let you in on the biggest challenges to his success early in your relationship. After all, you are there to solve or address those immediate problems. Coming into a programming department that is saddled with major difficulties gives you an immense advantage. You bring a fresh perspective, a creative approach, and a positive attitude that might be missing on the programming team. You may also bring application experience, programming expertise, and, of particular significance, the knowledge of appropriate programmer productivity tools that are very important to the company.

Over time, and with your demonstrated success as a programmer on his team, your manager will depend on you more and more, and eventually ask you to take on some high-profile projects for him. Recognize these cues and seize these opportunities. They are offered to star programmers on their way up.

The View from the Top

One of the marks of a bad programmer, says Theresa D'Alesandro, Director of Corporate Applications Development at Joe Cohill's company, is his or her lack of a broad perspective on the company's business operation.

"Good programmers go beyond the bounds of programming and learn the entire flow of business in their company," she says. "Bad programmers don't get to know, or want to know, the whole system; they

concentrate on their own little piece of it—say, printing a bill of lading. Seems simple enough: You press a button and the BOL is printed. However, there are all sorts of system processes that go on beyond the scenes when a BOL is printed. A simple change to the BOL may require a change to the manifest, the shipping label, the packing slip, or the invoicing files.

"How do I know this? Because I know the system. But many programmers become familiar with the process only when a modification is done to the program. And even then, the programmer's understanding is limited by the bounds of the program. This lack of understanding on the programmer's part may cause important processes not to take place—and that could translate into a customer's charging us back for a shipment not in compliance."

The compliance game itself is one of those flow-of-business processes about which Theresa expects programmers to be knowledgeable. These days, customers of almost any business routinely measure the quality, timeliness of delivery, and accuracy of products that a vendor ships to them against their purchase order. Your company will suffer serious consequences if you make a programming mistake that causes a shipment of goods to its client to fall out of "compliance." A failure to be perfect in every aspect of the distribution process can trigger punitive charge-backs (possibly as high as your yearly salary) for incorrect or late shipments.

"My job challenges me every day by testing my managerial and analytical skills," Theresa says. "I like working with other departments because it gives me a more complete view of how the company works.

"I expect the programmers I work with to question me about things: 'Why are we doing it this way?' Feedback from the programmers is very important. They can give another perspective that hadn't been considered. One of the most important things a manager can do is listen."

In short, Theresa expects her programmers to think like systems analysts—to know the industry in which their employer operates so they can intelligently apply their coding skills to whatever business problems they must solve. "When I give out a project, some programmers are in my office fifty times asking questions. The good programmers analyze the project, ask the few questions that need to be asked, and get it done. Why can they do it? Because they know the business! Instead of coming into my office with questions, they've learned the business on their own."

$$ The Bottom Line $$

From your first day on the job, focus on making your boss happy and promotable. That means not only diligently applying your coding skills but also working intelligently, having a consistent concern for accuracy, putting a lid on irritating questions, showing your boss respect, and, most important, doing your best to avoid presenting your boss with that management nightmare, the unpleasant surprise. All of these qualities will factor into your boss's evaluation of your work.

CHAPTER FOUR

Tips from a Technical Interviewer

When a programmer's in the midst of his design process, he's like an artist going to work on an empty canvas, or an architect when he takes a blank sheet of paper to design a new home.

W hen you are searching for a programming job, it is important to look at yourself through the eyes of a technical interviewer, because technical topics are sure to be a part of your interview. What qualities do you have, or what qualities should you hone, that will make you one of the favored applicants? Read on for the answer.

Advice You Can Use

Sam Gottlieb, a full-time programming consultant in New York City, is one of the many college English majors I've known who have built impressive programming careers. (Liberal-arts majors seem to doubt it, but you don't have to be a math whiz to become a splendid programmer.) For five years during the late nineties, Sam was manager of programming resources for a large software-consulting firm in New York City. He recruited programmers from around the world for assignments in the New York metropolitan area and was a technical manager involved in the design and coding of various projects. I asked him what impressed him most about the candidates whose credentials he was asked to judge.

"Assuming the technical skills I was looking for were there," he says, "I'd next look for communication skills. Could the applicant express himself well, verbally and in writing?"

Sam considered a candidate's knowledge of the particular business for which he was hiring another important credential. "If you know when you're in school that you want to program in a specific field—say, banking—it certainly makes sense to do whatever you can to learn about the industry," he says. As to education, Sam notes, "Most mature programmers I know never took any computer courses in school. It's just something they fell into. In the late nineties you could come out of school and get an entry-level job even with no programming or business experience." But, he acknowledges, the nineties were fat years for programmers. Now it's far different: "The business cycle has turned, as it always does, and right now we happen to be at the bottom. Now, even with a computer science degree, you're going to have a tough time getting a job as a programmer. Luck, timing, and—especially—contacts are the biggest factors in landing a job. The thing to remember is that demand for everything is cyclical; you're going to have boom times and bust times. But the market for programmers will revive.

"To get a job in this market, you have to satisfy every single requirement your prospective company has set. Today, in addition to good technical skills you are going to need business skills—you need to be knowledgeable about how a company operates. A few years ago, when programmers could practically name their price and companies couldn't be choosy, they'd bite the bullet and teach you about the business on the job. Now they hold out for exactly what they want—and business knowledge is a high priority."

Make Your Own Break

After an ambitious programmer has landed his first job, Sam advises, he should set out to learn new languages at work, and put in evenings and weekends trying to become better. That was the way he broke in.

"The first two years are the crucial years," he says. "If you can land that first job and hold on for between one and two years, you've got it made—assuming that you have the basic communication and personality skills. Once you've acquired two years of practical experience you should be able to switch companies and get a higher salary."

Sam's advice: These days, a programmer coming out of school has got to know either Java or Visual Basic. Then he can gravitate to whatever specific programming language his employer's IT department uses. Programmers will have more value if they are really good at one programming language than if they have a smattering of knowledge of several languages.

"You may not have to go to school at all. These days there are so many alternatives to sitting in a classroom to learn programming. You can pick up books like Teach Yourself Java *or* Teach Yourself C++ *in the Sam's series; it takes you step by step through the learning process on your computer."*

Sam doesn't believe that off-shore programmers are intrinsically better than American programmers: The off-shore and American programmers he's hired and worked with have the same range of ability and devotion to the work ethic, he says. But when Sam was a recruiter, legacy-language programmers were so desperately needed that his company also looked for programmers in other countries. And, he acknowledges, "Foreign programmers are less expensive, even when you count in the cost of sponsorship, because they'll take lower salaries.

"I'd get a list from our recruiting department of about fifteen people they wanted me to do technical interviews for," he notes. "Two might be in Ireland, four in Malaysia, three in Australia. Every now and then we contacted the people directly in those countries, on the basis of their résumé, a technical phone interview, and also trying to get a handle on how well they'd fit within the company.

"In those cases where the hiring was strictly by phone, I focused on the technical skills. In those phone interviews I was much more selective at the technical level. If I was sitting with someone across the table and I felt his technical skills were somewhat iffy but he had other qualities, I may have taken a chance on him. But when I did a phone interview and all the technical skills weren't there, I probably wouldn't have taken a chance.

"For a remote interview I'd prepare a list of questions, and I picked different ones to ask, depending on the interview. Also, if the candidate was unsure about the first question I'd ask in a specific area, I might ask more questions in that area. If not, I might skip to a different place."

Satisfaction Beyond the Salary

Like me, Sam Gottlieb relishes this work. But he acknowledges that a lot of people wouldn't. After my many years in the business, I have to agree with Sam. The money is great, but you have to know that you will be happy in this type of work. Let your résumé and cover letter show that you are in the industry for more than just a paycheck. It's that attitude that will carry you to your goals.

"It's a personality thing. I can try to explain the satisfaction of programming as articulately as I possibly can, but if someone doesn't think that sitting in a cubicle with a terminal for eight hours a day fits his personality, he is not going to find the job satisfying and creative. There's no way around that."

Sam continues: "When a programmer's in the midst of his design process he's like an artist going to work on an empty canvas, or an architect when he takes a blank sheet of paper to design a new home.

"There are many ways to design and write even the simplest program. The choices you make along the way will determine how well the program runs—how it looks, how it works, and how effectively it does what it's supposed to do. Those choices are what make programming creative and interesting.

"One of my clients was a very large clothing company with a huge warehouse down in North Carolina," Sam says. "Every week for six months I flew back and forth between New York and North Carolina as we set up an automated warehousing system for them. The merchandise came in on a huge conveyor system, and when the scanner hit the bar code of each carton, it indicated exactly what items were in that carton. The merchandise would be automatically added to inventory.

"One of the program's routines makes sure that a certain number of cartons—depending on the vendor—-are kicked aside for quality-control purposes. When we were all done and we had all this hardware and software working in conjunction, we stood on the platform and watched the truck pull up, taking these boxes and throwing them on the conveyor belt, and we saw the boxes going through the warehouse automatically, going on different tracks, some of them getting kicked off to the side, and it was a great thing."

$$ Bottom Line $$

Sam's perspective as a technical interviewer confirms my maxim "Come to a job interview armed not only with technical skill but with a knowledge of how a business works." In addition to that credential, Sam looked for the ability to solve problems calmly (an articulate job candidate should be able to convey that trait), the stated desire to learn new techniques, the willingness to keep up to date by reading widely in the field and in business, and the possession of good writing skills.

CHAPTER FIVE

Final Interview? Ask These Questions

*A good office setup will dramatically enhance your productivity. So
when you're on a job interview and you are asked whether you have
any concerns, you should ask some pointed questions.*

So, you made it through the multiple rounds of interviews and have
been offered a job. You should take it immediately, right? Wrong!
You still have to make sure it's the right job for you.

I know, I know. Turning down a job in any business climate is
tough to do, but you have to have the self-confidence to turn down a
job if you think it's the wrong job. You'd need to be convinced—as I
hope to convince you—that the wrong office environment can cripple
your ability to meet your manager's expectations, even if you push
yourself all day, every day. You must hold out for an ideal working
environment.

A good office setup will dramatically enhance your productivity. So
when you're on a job interview and you are asked whether you have
any concerns, you should ask some pointed questions.

Question 1: "What's My Access to the Computer?"

As you inspect your potential work area, inquire about the computer you'll be programming. How powerful is it? How limited or unlimited is your access to it? You don't care where the computer is, but
you need unfettered—that means virtually unlimited—access to maximize your programming productivity. Unfettered access means that
the computer is considered a corporate resource and you can do hundreds of program compiles day, if you need to. It also means that you

get immediate processing of your compiles—you don't languish in a job queue, waiting for processing of your job. Waiting in a queue means you are not productive, and that should not happen to programmers. If the company cannot afford a very fast computer, it probably cannot afford you.

Back in the old days—in the sixties—computers were so expensive that when a customer rented one, IBM threw programming help in free. Today, programmers are expensive and computers are cheap. Therefore, it's extremely important that the costly laborers—programmers, technicians, analysts, and consultants—have immediate and virtually unlimited access to the computer. Unless a programmer can do hundreds of test/compiles a day, he will find it impossible to accomplish the amount of work management expects him to accomplish.

So, on your walk through the office, ask whether you'll have free or restricted access to the computer. If you must wait around while someone else is using the machine, even because of production, you probably cannot succeed in that company. It's worth repeating: Before you take the job, make sure you'll have unfettered access to a fast computer. Without that, your productivity will be compromised. You may be a smart programmer, but you'll perform like a poor one. This can be dangerous to your financial health.

Question 2: "How Powerful Is the Computer?"

A powerful computer is one that provides virtually all of its online users with instant response time, rather than waiting for the screen to refresh with information. It provides very rapid processing of batch or submitted reports and programmer compiles.

I recently heard an IT datacenter manager tell some mainframe users who were coming onboard the corporate computer that he had some 4,000 interactive (online) users and they were all getting virtually instant response time. Program compiles are typically computer-intensive, but are now typically processed in seconds rather than in minutes (or even hours, as was the norm with older computers).

Question 3: "Where Will I Be Working?"

The ideal is to have your own office. The reality is that you will probably be working in the company of others. The former is a huge advantage. On the other hand, if you are shown a carrel on some busy floor where music is playing or an intercom is blaring, you know you're in trouble from the start, because you will not achieve the focus you'd have if your environment were quiet. That's why I wear earplugs on every client's premises when I am forced to sit in the bullpen.

Tell your interviewer you want to maximize your productivity, and that requires a quiet place. If your colleagues have a radio turned on or are listening to music through headphones, they are not being as productive as they could be—and the IT director obviously does not recognize the importance of a quiet work environment. And, of course, you don't want to be the one creating distractions. Don't bring in head-phones; don't listen to the radio. That will not only make you less effi-cient, but also will take an unfair toll on the attention-span of your colleagues.

Question 4: "Can I Minimize Distractions?"

Management too often worries about the cost per square foot of a private office rather than about the productivity-sapping consequences of noise and distraction. It is up to you to raise the issue. Even ear-plugs do not compensate for the chaos of the bullpen.

I bring the same programming capability, creativity, and will to ex-cel to every company I walk into. The company regulates my capacity to excel by means of the working conditions it presents me with. Those conditions, which are beyond my control, determine whether I will be superbly productive (and happy) or unproductive (and unhappy).

Of course, reality and budgets being what they are, you might not have the option of a private office. In fact, if you're already working in a cubicle, having your own office may seem like an impossible dream. But at the very least, you can have a serious talk with your manager about your need for a quiet environment. He or she can ban radios and speaker phones. When programmers start *demanding* quiet, smart managers will start providing it.

Question 5: "Will I Receive Strong Oversight?"

Your boss must ultimately be responsible for your work as a programmer.

> I once turned over to my manager a project that changed all six of the customer invoicing programs in a multi-billion-dollar company. The change was fairly minor, but there was a high risk that the company would not invoice millions of dollars if the change failed. I included comprehensive programming and test documentation with the project turnover to production, and I asked my programming manager to review it.
>
> Then I heard again the dreaded words: "Paul, I trust you."
>
> My boss most probably does have reason to trust my programming work, but even after fifty-two successful projects turned into production, I wanted the assurance of a review and inspection of my work by programming management.

It is all too easy for a programmer to misread, misunderstand, misinterpret, or miscode a project—which then causes disaster when it hits production. The programmer is there to do the work—high-quality work—but management is there to review, inspect, and take responsibility for it.

Your manager is ultimately responsible for your programming work and the consequences of your work. He needs to be able to coherently and effectively review your comprehensive project turnover material. If he doesn't do it, he should have someone else review your work and sign off on it. You are responsible for providing your manager with comprehensive project turnover material, including test results, and for being willing to review it with him before the project is put into production, not afterwards.

Question 6: "Is the Work Ethic Respected?"

In my opinion, too many programmers lack that old-fashioned virtue, the work ethic; that, I believe, may be one reason companies outsource their work to off-shore programmers or to domestic software support companies that take over the in-house IT department's function and prune out the slackers.

"In IT departments today, the nine-to-five programmers are becoming like the clerks of thirty to forty years ago," says Gene Bonett, founder and president of Xperia, a software development company in Allentown, Pennsylvania. "They've lost the desire to make the extra effort that's required to advance in this field.

"Unfortunately, the work ethic that was prevalent thirty years ago is prevalent today—but not with Americans," he says. "It's prevalent with programmers from India, China, and Russia. They're driving to become good. They want to be better than the Americans are, and they're eating our lunch.

"I feel strongly about this. When you stumble across Americans who have that old-fashioned work ethic, they shine. Our job at Xperia is to find as many of them as we can.

"The work ethic is more important to me than a guy who has a doctorate in computer science. I'll take a guy with the right attitude and a willingness to learn any day of the week—someone who wants to learn and who asks, 'Why do we do it this way?' Those kinds of employees are golden. You just don't find many of them.

"Many of the kids coming out of school today are coming out with unrealistic expectations. They seem to think, 'If I can write a batch program in school, then I should come out of school and move to the top of any organization I'm in.' But once you come out of school, your learning curve is just beginning. If you go in with the attitude that you're the lowest one on the list and you have a lot of ground to cover, you will do significantly better.

"The right attitude is vital. When I started, thirty years ago, there was camaraderie in this business, and a zealous attitude. There was a lot to learn, and people were dying to learn it; they put forth a major effort to master the job.

"Thirty years ago you could have walked into any IT department that I've been associated with on a Saturday or a Sunday, and 90

percent of the time you would have found a programmer there. Today, people have a tendency to run out the door at five o'clock.

"At Xperia, our normal hours are 8 a.m. to 5 p.m. But on a monthly basis we hold evening classes that start at 4:30 and run till 7. We do this to give people an understanding of the underlying technical structure of our system, of how the files relate, of the business itself. All of our programmers and trainees sit in on the in-house demos, and they're a part of the demonstration; they need to understand the questions people ask, because that's going to have an effect on their job.

"We do this to see who is interested in understanding and learning and who really doesn't care about it—just wants that job, wants to come in at 8 and leave at 5. That's okay, as long as the productivity levels within those hours are what we expect them to be. But we know that this programmer isn't going to advance. He isn't willing to put the extra effort into understanding his applications. He's not going to be able to service a customer at a customer site; he won't stay at the site till seven or eight o'clock, if that's what the job requires. If he won't do it in the office when he's on a training curve, then he'll never do it. And that attitude does affect his advancement and his pay.

"To me, the attitude and the approach that people take toward their job are the most important factors. I would rather take a marginal programmer with a tremendous attitude and a desire and willingness to learn than I would a super programmer who wants to sit there and do what he wants to do and come and go as he pleases."

What can we all learn from Gene's take on attitude? Attitude counts. Make sure you know the attitude of the shop you're going into. Ask about schedules and project time lines. Dig during the interview to find out if the team you are joining runs out the door at 5 p.m. or stays until the job is finished. You'll want to be on the latter team, because the latter team has the work ethic that leads to success. And then... make sure you share that ethic.

$$ The Bottom Line $$

Every programmer (and his manager) should pay attention to the career-crippling potential of a noisy environment and a slow computer. Indeed, I believe that a distracting environment or a slow computer will inevitably become so productivity-sapping that a job candidate should recognize this on his walk-through and turn the offer down. And make no mistake: Even in the twenty-first century—even in the foward-looking field of programming—an old-fashioned virtue, the work ethic, is still a prerequisite for success.

CHAPTER SIX

What You Won't Learn
in Programming School

"I've never been at a job where I've been stressed out. I've never gone home and said, 'I can't handle this.' There's nothing you can't work out or get help with. Don't allow yourself to believe that programming is going to be too hard for you."

A s you work hard in school and make the rounds in interviews, sometimes it's hard to visualize that programmers who are five or ten years ahead of you today were once in your shoes—looking for that first job, that first promotion, that first big break. If you get a chance to talk to these people—who are now where you want to be—you will learn a lot about the multiple paths to success. Toward that end, I give you the profile of Jason Honrath.

"I Play at Work"

"A lot of times people ask me what I do for a living," Jason says, "and I tell them, 'I play at work.' Programming is solving puzzles, and I enjoy working out puzzles—mastering problems. It's fun for me. When I come home from work, I know I've done something rewarding that day."

Jason is a 29-year-old programmer working at a small software development company outside Philadelphia. "People think programming is stressful, but that's not true. I've never been at a job where I've been stressed out. I've never gone home and said, 'I can't handle this.'

There's nothing you can't either work out or get help with. Don't allow yourself to believe that programming is going to be too hard for you. There's a popular misconception that programming is some kind of complex science, but it isn't. I know a lot of people, from all different backgrounds, who did poorly in high school and never would have thought of going to college, who went into programming and did well. I think that learning programming is not much harder than learning any other job."

Jason decided he wanted to be a programmer when he was in high school; he liked the Basic programming course he took in eleventh grade. After high school he spent several years driving a van for a uniform delivery company. When he got laid off after three years he decided to take programming seriously and enrolled in a nine-month course at the Cittone Institute, in Edison, New Jersey.

"I was kind of surprised," Jason says. "When I enrolled I expected it to be some really technical course with a lot of math and engineering, but it was basically like learning to do any other job, except a little more fun."

At Cittone he learned COBOL, RPG, CL (Control Language Programming), and Operations, all for the AS/400 (now iSeries) computer.

"I found it easy," Jason says. "I really enjoyed it. I learned enough in the nine-month course to get an entry-level job. At the job is where the learning really starts.

"It was pretty easy to get a job when I got out of Cittone, which was in 1995," he says. "After graduation the school wanted us to give them a list of companies we were interested in so the school staff could help us with the résumé and application process. But I wanted to look on my own. I used the newspaper and the phone book. I also used a book of companies (listed by state) that showed the type of computer they used and the name of the IT manager. My teacher let me copy the whole New Jersey section of the book. [You can find The Directory of Top Computer Executives, *a series of volumes listing the largest corporate computer shops in the United States—with hardware type, number of programmers, and name, address, and phone number of*

each shop's IT manager—in the business reference section of most major public or university libraries.]

"I sent out 25 or 30 résumés. Within a week I had my first interview. The ad in the newspaper said the company was looking for someone with two years' experience, but they called me anyway. I told the interviewers that it would take anyone—with or without experience—six months to learn the software anyway, and they could save money if they went with me. Bingo! Two days later I got a call from my teacher. The company had called him to check on my schooling, and had told my teacher they were going to make me an offer."

Surprise: It Takes More than Good Coding

Jason's new employer was a small company that had its own manufacturing and distribution packages written in COBOL, which they sold and supported, so Jason started in COBOL.

"My first challenge was my first big program. I had the coding down pat, but the business processes were all new to me. The big program I remember writing was a general ledger program, and I remember struggling with the concepts a lot. All I had learned in school was how to do the coding. But I did pick up the business concepts quickly. I remember going back about six months later, looking at some of my programs, and thinking how inefficient my coding was. I had learned more in six months of working than I had in nine months of school.

"In programming school I hadn't learned general ledger concepts or any other business processes. I don't know of any technical school that teaches you these business functions. My advice for people who want to go into programming is, take business courses. Whether you learn these business concepts in high school or college, they're far more important in your programming career than any math course. I do almost no math at work. The only thing math courses did for me was to sharpen my thinking skills.

"The business concepts I'd have found most useful to know when I started my job are accounting, work-in-process, bill-of-materials, inventory, receiving, and shipping. You don't have to learn these concepts in school, or even on the job. You can get simple books on them. You can also learn them on your PC with a generic software package that a small company would use for accounting or warehousing. Just

ask around to find a popular package that you'd find on the shelves of a retail computer store like CompUSA, and learn as much as you can. It will be more beneficial than anything else."

Jason left that company after a year. "I knew I could make a bigger salary if I moved around, because I knew people who were with the same company for a long time and their salaries hadn't grown as much as those of people I knew who were moving around. I caught on and switched jobs a couple of times in the next few years. My first jump gave me a 38 percent increase. When I left my second job I got a 48 percent increase. There is probably no other career in which someone who has not gone to college can advance so quickly in a couple of years.

"My second job was in an apparel company in Trenton. They were coding in RPG. I had taken it in school, but I had no job experience with the language. The company gave me a shot, since I did have experience with the business concepts they were using. When I was in school I didn't like RPG. I thought COBOL was the way to go. But after I worked with RPG, I realized that it was a lot easier to code. It seemed more efficient, and definitely made for faster coding.

"The company was small, with only one other person in the IT department. But this gave me a great chance to learn. I just got an RPG book and went at it. I was with this company for about a year before I made my second move, to my third job.

"This may not have been such a great idea, since my first two jobs were in the manufacturing and distribution environment and this job was with a payroll company. But the money was excellent, so I gave it a shot. After I was there for about six months, the company decided it was going to shift its focus to Internet applications. This led them to lay off most of their RPG staff and focus on Java. This was not the norm in business back then; it probably never would have happened in a manufacturing or distribution environment. As a matter of fact, a few months later, this payroll company was looking for RPG people to replace some of the programmers who had quit after the layoff, but RPG people were hard to find.

"Some of the payroll company's programmers got wind of the layoff before it happened, and that very same day there was a recruiter out in the parking lot trying to hire consultants.

"I got laid off at the end of October. I didn't bother opening a newspaper. I just called the agency that had gotten me the job with the *payroll company. In two weeks I had three offers, two in writing and one verbal. Three offers in two weeks!"*

College is Only One Credential

A popular misconception is that you have to go to college to make a lot of money in programming, but Jason maintains that it is not so.

"I am not saying that a degree is not helpful," Jason says. "What I am saying is that it is not at the top of most IT managers' list of credentials for an entry-level programmer. I believe that on-the-job experience is worth a lot more than a college education. I could tear up my diploma from technical school, and probably high school, too," Jason says. "As long as I can program, I'll have a job. The only negative thing a younger programmer might run into is older programmers who have been with the company for a long time. Sometimes they don't like the fact that a young person with no college education can walk in and get a very competitive salary. But just keep in mind that if you can do the programming, you deserve the job as much as anyone else."

Write New Programs—Make More Money

There are two—sometimes three—main aspects to an entry-level programming job, Jason points out.

"The first is program maintenance, which is making modifications to programs that were written by somebody else. The second is writing new programs, using specs provided by a systems analyst or programmer/analyst. And, third, a young programmer might get to work directly with a user, designing the specs for a new program.

"Chances are that a lot of your work as a young programmer will be the maintenance of programs. This is the least desirable, because writing new programs and designing new programs will give you much more experience much faster. A programmer with a year's experience writing brand-new programs will probably be more knowledgeable than someone who spent two years doing maintenance.

"Still, even though a new programmer has to do a lot of maintenance, it is possible to get a job in which you can spend some time

writing new programs—or even working with end users, designing programs. The best way to do this is to go to work at a smaller company rather than a big one. You may make a little less money at first, but the experience will be excellent. The entry-level programmer who goes into a shop with two or three programmers will have more programming responsibility than someone in a company with a programming staff of 100, and therefore will learn more.

"Do not take a job in which you will be maintaining programs for three years, or writing only print programs. In the interview, ask what your responsibilities will be. You want to be spending at least some of your time on new programs. Also, a job where you will get to work with users or clients is an excellent opportunity. It will be challenging but also rewarding.

"Another thing to look for in your first job," Jason says, "is a company that is using mainstream software—a package used by other companies that are in the same type of business. Use the Internet, newspapers, or magazines to find out what kinds of software packages are in use by a lot of companies. Experience with a particular package can be more valuable than experience in a particular language."

How to Become a Marketable Programmer

Jason feels that it is important to sell yourself, even if you aren't sure what an IT manager is looking for in terms of skills.

"Make sure you present yourself well," Jason recommends. "Chances are that the manager will be looking at your verbal skills, since communication is a big part of programming." Jason agrees with Gene Bonett that it's important to show your boss that you'll be a zealous worker: "You must have an eager attitude toward learning.

"Send lots of résumés. Ads on the Internet or in the newspaper are an excellent source of jobs. Even if the ad calls for two years' experience or sounds as if it pays too much money for your qualifications, send the résumé anyway. Chances are that the company might have an entry-level opening soon; this is a fast-moving business. I sent résumés out to companies looking for ten years' experience. Also, the company staffer who placed the ad might know someone at another firm who is looking for a programmer at your level. Make sure you call the company a week after you've sent the résumé. This is to make sure

they got it. Well, it is also forces them to remember your name, and if they have to look for your résumé, it will now be on top.

"As you move from job to job, which you will if you want to increase your salary quickly, there are things you should keep in mind. This is a business where a paycheck isn't the only thing you get from a job. You also get an education. Try to learn from people there. Take advantage of books they have and people that are above you. Find someone there that you can use as a mentor and become his or her friend. They could do you a lot of good. Also, try to get in on as many big projects as you can. If you are doing all maintenance after six months, tell your boss that your skill level is now good enough to enable you to write new programs. The key to learning is writing new programs, important programs.

"The programmer who is happy changing the headings on all of the reports in the company, or standardizing display file colors and function keys for five years, will probably be doing the same thing until he retires.

"And always show a good work ethic. Work hard and show up all the time. Make friends with co-workers, bosses, and clients. When you leave a company, leave on the best terms you can. Make sure you give notice. Your new employers will respect you for making them wait two or three weeks instead of just walking out on your old company.

"I have friends who have worked for software vendors, and later on went to work for one of the vendor's clients because they knew the package well. I have friends who worked for a company and went on to work for that company's software vendors. I have had bosses who left companies I was working for to go somewhere else, and when they got there, they called me with a job offer.

"These opportunities will definitely happen when you treat your employer right. If you walk out without notice or don't work hard for them, down the road you will apply for a job, and guess who will be working there? Your old boss. Market yourself well and make a lot of friends; they will help you in the future."

After learning Java on his own time, Jason landed a more challenging, more creative job, at a substantial salary increase, at a small software company outside Philadelphia.

"They were looking for someone with solid RPG experience who could write Java and HTML," he says. "I like working for a smaller company; I get a lot more exposure here. And now I get to work with RPG, Java functions, Web stuff, WebSphere . . . It takes a more complex set of skills to know three or four different technologies. Change is good."

When he left his old firm, Jason gave three weeks' notice, and his colleagues and managers gave him a farewell luncheon. He did what he advises other programmers to do: He left them smiling.

$$ The Bottom Line $$

If you're a fledgling programmer who's afraid to leave a job that bores you, or who believes there are projects you can't master, Jason's exuberance and self-confidence should be a bracing tonic. His tips on how to look for work, how to impress an interviewer, and how to acquire the business knowledge you need should bolster your own self-confidence, whether you venture out of your present job or stay where you are and reach for more complex projects to tackle.

CHAPTER SEVEN

The Beauty of Borrowed Code

Painters and writers yearn to be original—to express their ideas in a new way. In writing code, however, originality is not usually an asset; following corporate standards is.

You are making a big leap when you go from computer school to a corporate programming job. In school you have been passive, for the most part—learning from the instructor and reading books. (Of course, you've done some minimal exercises, written simple programs in the computer labs, taken tests, and gotten help when you asked for it.)

Now that you have a corporate programming job, you are expected to be active—productive enough to justify the nice salary you are earning. In fact, once you've passed the trainee stage, your company will look on you as the answer-man or answer-woman; you are not supposed to be going to other programmers for help all the time.

New programmers driving to produce on their first job are well aware that their way of coding might not be the best way. They know their work may be at times clumsy and inefficient. What they probably do not suspect, however, is how powerful they can instantly become simply by borrowing the code of a programmer in their shop who writes elegantly and smartly.

Painters and writers yearn to be original—to express their ideas in a new way. In writing code, however, originality is not usually an asset; following corporate standards is.

Tap into an Expert's Brain

The greatest productivity multiplier for programmers is a fast and continually available computer. The second-greatest productivity multiplier is simply to copy code.

You, a corporate programmer, have available to you, in the millions of lines of production source code in your company's source program libraries, a treasure-trove of proven and tested source programs, routines, and functions. All you have to do is use these existing blocks of source code to your advantage—and your company's benefit. First you learn what that existing source does, and then you copy appropriate blocks of proven and tested existing source code into your programs. What the existing production source code does is define and execute all the critical business processes in your company

A programmer who doesn't work smart might write 200 lines of code a day (of source statements), perhaps taking ten days to write a routine 2,000-statement program (about 40 pages) from scratch. He would then still face the daunting task of making it work. Programmers who work smart by using their experience and modeling their programs from code that has been written for a similar project might create a program that achieves the same objective, test it, and have it ready for client review—perhaps even ready for production—in less than one day.

You need to be that smart programmer.

I advise you to review the production source code that is now running computing for your company. You'll find it in your company's production source library. Then use the technique that I and every other successful programmer I know use constantly: Copy the (non-copyrighted) code of someone who has done a good job on a similar function or project.

Even if the programmer who wrote the code you are working on has moved to another job, you can learn from his work—and see the code's results in a production environment. I learn the most by (1) observing the output of the executing program, then (2) reviewing the source program techniques and code that produced the results. I work backward from the result: I look at the answer to learn how the solution was developed.

A good programmer never really starts from scratch. He brings to the project his own thoughts, but he'll also put into his program blocks of code that other programmers have created—just as a cook often uses canned chicken broth rather than going to the labor of making her own stock. (Programming is different from cooking in this way: Homemade chicken stock tastes better than canned broth, but "canned" code—the code you copy—is usually better than any code an inexperienced programmer can write from scratch.)

Corporate programmers are not paid to invent completely new programs; they are paid to support the company business goals as productively as they can. Remember this and you will prosper.

Why Reinvent the Wheel?

I learned just how powerful a technique the copying of large blocks of source code can be thirty years ago, when I was a systems engineer at IBM. My colleague, Garry Reinhard—the most talented programmer I have ever seen in action—was working with me to develop the first online software package ever created for the apparel industry (IBM would eventually name it the Apparel Business System).

We were running a marathon for months. Not only did our programming work last into the evening hours seven days a week, but we were forced to do keypunching too. (Our team secretary didn't know how.) So, after we had done the coding, we had to keypunch our programs into IBM punched cards and run them through a card reader on the IBM System/370 mainframe.

This was laborious, because there were no online terminals; we had to key the entire source program for, say, customer master file maintenance into 80-column punch cards, then compile and test it. This we did at night at the IBM data center after the IBM customers went home to dinner.

Because we had no online source statement editor (to catch keypunching errors or programming syntax), undetected errors, as well as the slow mainframe compile times of the early seventies, made even relatively simple programs take a long time to complete. We had to wait until the next night to correct the simplest error.

Garry quickly discovered that all of the master files we used in our software package, such as the customer master, the style (or product) master, and the employee master, used almost exactly the same programming techniques for as much as 90 percent of the programs. So did files with header and detail records, such as the customer order file, the accounts receivable file, and the work-in-process file. Nearly the only changes needed in the programs were the file names and the fields used in each application, and some validation editing of the fields.

Garry produced an incredible amount of completed and working programs in a very short time by reproducing the completed Assembler source program deck (copying the source program) and making the minor changes needed for the next master file maintenance. This method sounds simple—the obvious thing to do—but back then, few programmers worked that way. Garry had to find a very productive way to work so that we could make our product delivery schedule with a quality product, and he had to do all the work himself.

The technique Garry came up with to dramatically raise his productivity thirty years ago is just as available to smart programmers today: Indeed, copying is the basis of many of the software tools that claim to multiply programmer productivity. The task is surprisingly simple: Find what is wasting much of your time and frustrating you, then look in your company library for already-invented code that takes care of the problem.

Copy Code, but Build Your Own Sound Design

In programming school, you worked on throwaway programs, used once for your education. Your tests simply allowed your teacher to evaluate your work. When you're on the job, however, the programs you write are expected to drive the corporation's business processes and provide the company with a competitive edge and happy, efficient end users.

Some of the programs that I and other programmers have written have been used in production for twenty-five years or more; they've been executed millions of times. A typical production program will be used for at least several years, and over its lifetime, it will be maintained and enhanced by many programmers. Therefore, the first requirement in corporate production programming is a sound design. Follow that with accurate and precise programming, testing, implementation, and support of the business function or project.

I go to almost any length to document my source programs accurately and precisely with comments (non-executable statements) so that the programmers who follow me will find it easy to understand the program objectives, processing flow, and functions of the blocks of code in the program. The end user never sees this extra effort, but the success of the many programmers who will follow me in maintaining the program often depends on it. When I see few or no comments in a complex program, or misspelled words—or, even worse, incorrect documentation and "dead" (obsolete, unused) code, I am immediately wary of the quality of this programmer's executable source statements, and that calls his programming ability into question.

Don't Wing It!

"What do I do now?" "How do I do this?" "How can I minimize my risk?" "Why isn't it working?" These questions have passed through the mind of every beginning programmer. My first suggestion is, "Do not wing it; do not guess." Corporate programmers who continually choose to guess, wing it, or take a hip shot for the design rather than using the tools and information available to them are a (deservedly) vanishing breed.

Even the most talented programmer cannot look up at the ceiling and spin through millions of lines of code to imagine what would happen under any possible condition. Yet many programmers try to do just that, rather than take a well-planned, proven, orderly and certain path toward a sound design for solving complex problems.

All of the techniques you need to avoid winging it have doubtless been invented and refined; they've appeared in some IT magazine, book, or software product available to your company, or been invented by your colleagues in the IT department. Now these techniques are being used by the most successful programmers in your company. So you must, first, observe how your successful colleagues have solved the very same problem you've been presented with. Then you will form your design, determining not to ask for too much help from anyone.

How to Find Reusable Code

You have undoubtedly heard much about object-oriented coding and object-oriented programming languages. Smart, productive programmers have always taken a fundamental goal of object-oriented programming—reusable, executable code—to its logical extreme: They consider every line of any source program as potentially available for reuse, so that re-coding can be avoided. You can easily find the entire prior programming done in your company by using the powerful Find functions available on almost all corporate computers. Then you can copy this code into other source programs.

For the forty years that I have been programming, objects performing standard functions have always been called as sub-programs by the calling program needing that function. The technique of copybooks (copying blocks of source code into a source program) or calling executable program objects (compiled source programs) in a source program has been around and effective since programs were first written. The savvy programmer copies not only huge blocks of source code but even a single source statement that he needs. In doing so he acquires proven code for himself, greatly multiplies his own productivity, and enhances the quality of the finished program.

Do not let anyone's definition of what an object is, or what object-oriented programming is, deter you from copying much or even most of your program's code. Copying all the source code you can is simply smart. This vital technique will propel you toward success as you learn from the efforts of others.

Warning, warning, warning: You should not copy or reproduce copyrighted code. Nevertheless, you can learn from—and greatly benefit from—sound programming techniques used in copyrighted code. Automobile designers and manufacturers buy a competitor's car and strip it down to learn from it. Similarly, you can learn much from the programming of similar functions that someone more experienced and skilled than you are has already done.

Even with Borrowed Code, You Need to Test, Test, Test

My experience is that a programmer will spend about 25 percent of his time on analyzing and planning a project or program. He will then spend about 50 percent of the time on a project in actual coding, which is simply translating his solution to the business process into one or more source programs in an appropriate programming language. The remaining 25 percent of the project or program time should be spent in very careful and comprehensive testing and system testing with representative test data that really exercises all of the known and anticipated program functions. What you should do is provide your manager with testing that includes the details that prove the correctness of your changes, not just your answer.

$$ The Bottom Line $$

The savvy programmer becomes super-productive by copying not only huge blocks of source code, but also single source statements that he needs. So, do the smart thing: copy, copy, copy (not to mention test, test, test). And never try to wing it.

CHAPTER EIGHT

Learning from the Masters

*Whether you're on your first job or you're an experienced program-
mer who has jumped to a new job, your mission should be to learn
who the best programmer in your company is and then model your
work on his (or hers).*

Programming mistakes can have serious consequences for your
company. The experienced programmer to whom I recently acted
as mentor was anxiously alert to his power to bring on disaster just by
doing his everyday job. Having left programming to work in factory
distribution years before, he was just returning to programming, after
taking a refresher course. He was (rightly) intimidated by the fact that
his programming changes would affect hundreds of online users who
depended on the applications. Twenty years ago, his exposure to programming errors was limited—say, to a single user reviewing a
printed report.

"What do I do?" my mentee asked me. "Just how do I do this? I was
a good programmer before, but I'm lost in picking up a complex and
very large application. What's in these huge, sophisticated programs?
How can I minimize my risk?"

He was not only asking the right questions, he was sensibly afraid
of making mistakes that would adversely impact hundreds of online
users, stopping them from doing productive work. You should be asking the same questions.

In this chapter, I'll share some of the important advice I gave him.

Don't Split the Business Logic

Today's corporate programs are quite large, primarily because the typical business function being automated—say, using Radio Frequency barcode to wand units into cartons in a distribution center—is a complex job requiring several thousands of lines of source code. It is simply easier, and perhaps more effective, for the programmer to put all of the core or mainline programming logic that implements the business function into one large program than it is to split the business logic into many fragmented pieces and programs. That's not what they teach you in IT school, but that's the way it really works in corporate programming.

The programmer should not split one logical program of a business function into 50 parts, calling the 50 sub-programs from the main program and then having the called programs call more programs down many levels (in the call stack). If the business logic, such as validating a customer number, is truly unique to the program, then put it in the program, not in a sub-program. My mentee was faced with supporting a complex, vendor-supplied package that had up to eleven levels of called programs (in which each program calls another program, which calls another program—the process repeating eleven times). He was (understandably) mystified, even as to which program was being executed.

My answer to my mentee's question "What do I do now?" was to show him some simple auditing techniques that helped him deal with the complexity of the programs he had to change. (You'll find those techniques in Chapter 16, "Master Millions of Lines of Complex Code.") Then I showed him how to use the computer's Find function to search through millions of lines of his company's production source code to find how another programmer had solved the same problem.

Cloning the Brain of a Programming Master

The key piece of advice I gave my mentee was this: "Search your company's production source program library for the portfolio of the best programmer at your company—the programmer you want to model yourself after. (Use FInd to search by his or her name. You can also, of course, use FInd to search for any program, file, or field name.)

Whether you are on your first job or you're an experienced programmer who has jumped to a new job, your mission is to learn who the best programmer in your company is, find a programming style that works for you, and copy that style. What was successful for the best programmer in the company—and understandable to you—will enlighten you.

Select some of the master's programs and see how he or she handled a task similar to the one you're tackling. If you use this technique, you will quickly become a very good, fast programmer.

For this training session, I chose a master my colleague might want to emulate . . .well, me. We used the Find function to search all of the source programs containing the word HARKINS in the company's production source program library. That brought up all the programs that I had written or maintained that were in production. We chose a dozen or so programs that were similar to the project that he had been assigned to do.

Now he could review each program description to see what business process the program addressed. Then he could see every line of code that I had written or changed, and, since I put extensive comments into my source code for the benefit of the programmers who came after me, my mentee could see my comments too. He could see the specifications of the program, the major programming steps (or pseudo code) of each function, the modifications that were requested, and a detailed description of each processing step. So all he had to do was find those programs and look at them online.

Looking at my source code, or any other programmer's source code, is like getting the answers to a test. My mentee could study my code and my technique, and know that it actually worked. He could then adapt those techniques and use that style in his own programs. And he could have very high confidence that the program he was writing would work. If he had a question, he could come back to me and I would understand what he was trying to do, because he was using the style I used. (If he were using a different style or struggling with his own style, it would take a lot more time to help him—time I might not be able to spare.)

My mentee reviewed my work, read my comments, and became familiar with my programming style. This gave him the confidence to get started, and he soon began accumulating a portfolio of his own successful techniques for use in later programs.

Why Delete Your Safety Net?

I advised my mentee to save both the current production source and object programs and to pilot-test his project before he committed it to production.

Saving both the current program source code and the program executable object program almost always allows for rapid recovery of a failed programming change by using procedures found in the project implementation turnover documentation. Many programmers do not bother to save the current production executable object program before overlaying it with the new object program, thinking that they can quickly recompile the saved source program. Then they find out that they cannot easily re-create the object program when the new one fails, because something is not exactly the same as it was long ago when the original executable object program was last compiled—perhaps disk file format changes, or a library list error where the incorrect libraries and disk file are referenced. That causes intense and unnecessary stress on the programmer from IT management and the end users. I have seen programmers lose it when they cannot figure out what is wrong when a project backout is required.

Pilot That Program

Next, I showed him how to test and then "pilot" his changes with a single user in a production environment. Piloting a critical new or changed application (limiting the number of production users to a single user and monitoring the results) closely replicated the environment he worked in twenty years ago, in a much simpler programming world. When he learned that he could test for errors the old-fashioned way, with a single user, rather than "live," where the program would affect hundreds of users, he quickly gained confidence. Pilot testing is crucial in testing and implementing key applications that can shut down the company and generate calls to the IT VP from top management.

Piloting your project implementation means testing it with a single lead user (pilot user), rather than "going live" and finding out that the program you just wrote or changed has stopped 3,000 cartons of critical shipments dead on the warehouse conveyor, and now the packers barcode-scanning the items into cartons must stop also.

The pilot user typically accesses the new code by using a pilot sign-on while using the existing production databases. This allows the programmer to focus on a key user for feedback about problems or for suggestions about the changed business process—far more agreeable than being overwhelmed by hundreds or thousands of vocal users who cannot do their job anymore. These outraged users generally call the programmer after first calling their manager about this new IT problem.

Pilot production lets the programmer and his manager implement very complex and high-risk programming projects much more quickly and successfully. That's because the risk can be focused on one observable, competent end user, rather than on the entire user community. I will not implement a complex, high-risk, high visibility programming project without piloting it first.

$$ The Bottom Line $$

Emulate the style, techniques, and general approach to programming that have worked for the best of your colleagues. Modeling yourself on a master will swiftly boost you and your career toward success.

CHAPTER NINE

Techies and Bit-Twiddlers Are Doomed

The smart corporate programmer will use the simplest, most basic program code to implement his projects, reserving his intense focus for the business function being developed.

Your job as a corporate programmer is to produce programs that will improve the productivity of your company—save it money or make it money. You were hired to improve corporate business processes in the most straightforward, productive way, not to come up with fancy-for-fancy's-sake coding techniques. This message is so fundamental to the success of corporate programmers that it deserves a separate chapter in this book.

Corporate programming means implementing practical business tasks—automating business functions and helping end users access corporate IT systems. Why, then, do so many business programmers turn out convoluted code, as if they were visionaries hired to guide spaceships around a galaxy?

They do it, I suspect, for the same reason that academics turn out unreadable prose—to show how "intellectual" they are. This is bad writing, both in English and in computer code. My counsel to all corporate programmers is this: Do not try to make programming into a mystique. Focus on increasing your understanding of corporate business processes (applications) and then do your programming with minimal complexity. Indeed, make a conscious decision to write your code as straightforwardly as you can.

Keep It Simple

Over my long career, I have written thousands of corporate programs. In 99 percent of them—programs created in many different languages, for hundreds of different companies—I've had to use only a very limited set of instructions: READ, WRITE, ADD, SUBTRACT, MULTIPLY, DIVIDE, MOVE, IF, PERFORM. Just those, and perhaps fifty additional instructions of similar simplicity. Computer languages do contain hundreds of additional, complex instructions, but they are rarely, if ever, used—at least by me and by most corporate programmers. Sometimes I wonder why they were ever put into the language.

Yes, you can probably find a way to utilize almost every complex instruction in your source program, but the people who follow you will pay the price—and perhaps you will pay the price, too, in making something that really is simple into something complex. Complex, hard-to-maintain programs cost the company money, for they waste the time of the programmer who has to puzzle them out.

I include the following illustration of the fundamental structure of corporate programs for those readers who are not yet corporate programmers, and for those corporate programmers who have not yet grasped the virtue of keeping it simple.

To a non-programmer, code looks perplexing. And yet, given a short course in its grammar and syntax, the non-programmer can interpret the code. Take this sentence: "If it's sunny Wednesday, let's go to the beach. But if it's not sunny, let's go to the movies." The COBOL "code" for that might be "IF SUNNY WEDNESDAY, GO TO BEACH, ELSE GO TO MOVIES."

If you were to code that sentence in RPG, the sentence might read like this:

```
WED          IFEQ        SUNNY
             GOTO        BEACH
             ELSE
             GOTO        MOVIES
             END
```

This is not particle physics. Now—full disclosure—you won't be writing code about the beach and movies; you'll be writing code that tells the computer how to check inventory records, or cut a velvet dress, or load merchandise into cartons. And there will be some code-like symbols. But they're easily learned.

Virtually all corporate programming—across all hardware platforms and across all programming languages (at least the fifteen or so languages in which I have been paid to program) —is based on the simple elements of a condition (IF) followed by an action (GOTO). Those programmers who are offended by using a GOTO, or GO TO, may ITER to the beach.

So, basically, if you can think somewhat logically (for instance, not writing; "IF it RAINS THEN GOTO the BEACH"), then you can probably be a good corporate programmer. The programming conditional IF statement is simply an English question whose answer is "true" (THEN), or "false" (ELSE). Corporate programming really doesn't get much harder than that.

Bit-Twiddlers Get (and Deserve) No Glory

The most successful corporate programmers, and their IT managers, have earned their promotions and their high compensation by their success in implementing critical projects that solve business needs. Their work shines through the output that the end user and corporate management can see; the improvement in productivity the programmer produced can probably be measured as return-on-investment or payback for the IT development work. Unlike techies, these productive programmers are truly creative; they find ingenious solutions to a problem when other programmers are stymied. But they do not doodle away the day foolishly trying new ways to solve a simple problem.

A grand total of zero end users and top corporate managers will ever look at the program code used to implement that improved business function and marvel at your coding ability. The end user doesn't know and doesn't care what your programs look like, as long as they get the needed jobs done. The smart corporate programmer will use the simplest, most basic program code to implement his projects, reserving his intense focus for the business function being developed.

I have watched techie programmers spend days, weeks, months developing a fantastic array of programming tricks and sophisticated techniques when they could (and should) have been tackling available high-visibility and creative corporate IT projects that might save the company millions of dollars. Then the techie wonders why the non-techie programmer and his manager who work on those high-visibility (and sometimes high-risk) projects got promoted. And while the techie is straining his creativity on routine tasks, thousands of other techie programmers around the world may be developing the same clever techniques—leaving him just an average techie programmer after all.

Your programming manager is most probably not as good a programming technician as you are. And the VP of IT and the senior programmers in your IT department are most probably not as technically adept at programming as you are. That should provide an indication that it's not technical skills that will get you to the top. Put another way, excellent technical car mechanics spend all day under cars on lifts and getting greasy, while the used car manager makes a fortune with his knowledge of how well the cars on his lot run. It doesn't seem fair, but literal technical knowledge is almost never rewarded very highly, perhaps because it is too easily learned.

Most of the techie programmers I have worked with are not particularly creative; they focus instead on fanatically working to extend the known published programming functions to often fantastic lengths. For instance, every programming language has a number or operators, or operation codes, or functions that trigger the computer to do something—like ADD and SUBTRACT. Virtually all of these operators have a list of required or optional parameters that can be utilized. Sometimes the parameters may take a full page of a manual to describe. The techie programmer will take it as a personal challenge to learn, test, and eventually use in his programs as many of the operators and their parameters as he can. Having mastered every operator in the language, he often then creates some "nifty" commands or new functions not already available in the programming language and then leaves the company, leaving his ingenuity to waste other programmer's time.

Focusing on learning every programming language operator and its parameters and then using them all is, I think, very foolish—something like learning all the words in a dictionary and finding a use for each of them. It would be far better to select a few useful words and creatively string them together into a significant document.

Technical Skills Can Do You Wrong

And make sure that possessing certain technical skills doesn't hold you back. You may need to "lose" those skills. One day while I was at IBM as a senior systems engineer, my SE manager called me in to review my annual programming skills report. IBM kept a skills inventory of each employee and had the employee and his manager update it annually. That allowed IBM to match employees with needed support requirements. It also helped managers determine the level of an employee's technical competence and decide whether he needed more education in a specialty.

My manager wanted to know what had happened to my previously listed technical competency in the IBM System/370 CICS macro-level Assembler language, because he had a need for that skill. I told him, "gone forever." I had a plan to move on and up, and keeping up old technical skills would have stopped that from happening.

The Rewards of True Creativity Are Many

A programmer should focus his creative talent on finding an elegant solution to the business problem he's addressing, not to fussing around with computer code. This takes more time and mental effort than journeyman programmers are willing to expend: Most programmers stop at a basic solution. But superior programmers keep turning the problem over in their mind, wondering, "Can I come up with a better solution?" They are like writers refining their prose, like artists painting the scene over and over, to make it better. And this is necessary when you're dealing with a complex job like automating a warehouse with a sophisticated system to pick full cases. Basic solutions won't work for big, mission-critical jobs.

Whenever I write new code, I am an inventor—I create a unique programming solution. No other programmer will handle the parameters and constraints of the job as I will; no one else will take the steps I take to implement the application. This—finding an elegant solution to a business problem—is creative work, and doing it well has buoyed me over a career lifetime.

Sometimes the job is unmistakably important (like, say, keeping planes from colliding, or running a bank's ATM machines, or guiding the computers used in surgery). Even less glamorous projects, though, are brain-challengers, and there is satisfaction in creating a smoothly running operation that does something useful. Thirty-five years ago, I automated the fabric-cutting operation of an apparel company. My job was to do a much better and faster job than the six experienced cut planners could do—and greatly improve the company's capacity to estimate fabric and cutting labor costs precisely. It was a not a glamorous job like keeping an airplane flying, but there was a reward in doing it well. That program cost perhaps $10,000 to write, but it saved the company millions of dollars as it planned and optimized the utilization of expensive men's suiting fabric and cutting-room labor in the cutting of millions of suits. Apparently, no one was able to improve upon this "tightly written code," because that program ran for twenty-five years, until the company went out of business.

$$ The Bottom Line $$

There are many multi-million-dollar programming projects waiting to be discovered by corporate programmers who will ride those opportunities to glory. Go after those projects; don't waste your corporate career as a bit-twiddler. Inventing complex ways to perform a simple task and turning routine code into a showcase for your inventiveness will bring you no reward except the label "unproductive techie."

Section 2

Thriving in a Competitive Environment

Stay-in-Front Strategies for Seasoned Professionals

CHAPTER TEN

Harnessing the "Brute Force" of Calculation

Reviewing your source code as you wrote it, without compiling it, is almost always a very big waste of time, because only the program compile is the final judge of whether your code is correct enough to create an object program.

The computer can make you incredibly smart—if you let it. However, many of the programmers I've observed over the years, in many different IT departments, actually refuse the computer's help.

I still see programmers—almost always journeyman programmers—listing their source programs for review and then poring over their own code as if they had not just written it. That drives me crazy. It is as if they are purposely working in slow motion, afraid to have the computer see their errors.

Well, the computer really does not care about you or your coding. It simply tells you the truth, so why delay the news?

Save Your Brain

Journeyman programmers burn their brains trying to do the work that is best done by the computer, and they never succeed with their real job, which is focusing on creative programming and programming logic, rather than wasting their time on programming details—details that should be automatic. For writers, the instant spell-check and grammar-check available at the push of a button on a Mac or PC frees time for content rather than for mechanics. Programmers should utilize the compiler in exactly the same way.

You have at your fingertips——literally—the biggest productivity multiplier since the harnessing of electricity.

In 1992, five years after chess Grandmaster Garry Kasparov lost a tournament to IBM's supercomputer "Deep Blue," he lamented to *The New York Times* that what he had been up against was "the brute force of calculation." And indeed he was. Happily, the "brute force" is with you, not against you. You can harness it. So let the computer show you how successful your latest code is, while you are taking a mental break and preparing for your next block of creative programming.

Never just list your source program on a printer and review the source code you have keyed as the source program. Reviewing your source code as you wrote it, without compiling it, is almost always a very big waste of time, because only the program compile is the final judge of whether your code is correct enough to create an object program. A successful program compile also allows your program logic to be tested with data—testing you should do with virtually every small block of programming.

In the early days of computing, we had serious limitations on the design and implementation of projects because our computing power was very slow (often allowing only one compile a day, or more precisely, at night, after the prime production computer shift).The source programs were keypunched into decks of punched cards rather than stored on disk, and we worked with computer printouts rather than with online display terminals. Just to change a single line of source code, we might have to spend five minutes to read the source program card deck into the computer with the card reader before the sometimes hour-long process would even start. Then it would take several minutes for the printer to print the results of the compile before we would know if our change had errors. Today, that entire process might be condensed into ten seconds—the time it takes to determine and act on the results of a program compile.

Sometimes we would write a program that would randomly access tens of thousands of disk records. We'd get really alarmed when the disk drive rocked back and forth slightly as the disk arm raced back and forth across the 10-inch or 14-inch disk platters. Today, the disk drives are buried inside some computer cabinet, the disk platters are one or two inches long, and the "read" and "write" mechanisms float over the disks so quietly that programmers are unaware of how many million disk-record accesses are taking place. And, for the most part, programmers don't need to care about it.

It is almost comical, at least to me, to observe programmer "techies" working so hard and long to save nanoseconds in a program rather than focusing on the business process of the project. They justify their work as being efficient—and yet they run the entire program only once a week, though it executes in one computer (CPU) second.

Beware the Queue

But the instant response time your company's computer system provides is of no value to you if the company requires your programming work to go behind production work in the computer queue. When you submit a program for a compile, it should immediately become active; you should get the results within seconds. If your compile-submitted jobs are languishing behind any other jobs in any queue, then you, too, are languishing—being unproductive.

> Queuing theory ("the study of the queue as a technique for managing processes and objects in a computer," according to Google.com) runs a whole lot of the world—and particularly the computer world. I was introduced to the theory decades ago at IBM's Systems Research Institute in New York. Our class was taught by a brilliant young teacher named Shelly. He spent weeks drawing complex queuing-theory equations on the blackboards on all three sides of the classroom while discussing the merits of single vs. multi-server queues.
>
> His students—particularly me—cringed, awaiting the fateful final examination. Then, when almost everyone except the students from the IBM laboratories was in despair, Shelly said; "Your final exam is to go down to the Dime Savings Bank and observe why they use a single

queue of people served by many tellers, rather than a queue of people lined up before each teller." As I remember it, we all celebrated that evening because we had learned the essentials of queuing theory, which is to find and implement strategies that will avoid or minimize queues (waiting).

As a corporate programmer, you must avoid queues in your project design and in your work environment. This can be as basic as keeping your archived output (printer) queue free from old information that you will never want to review again. You shouldn't be wasting time looking through old information; your focus should be only on current information. When you're confronted with a queue, find a way around it

Unfortunately, finding a way around a queue won't always be as easy as keeping your printer queue free of old data. You may have to challenge company policy to get your work to the front of the queue. However, the stakes for your career are so high that addressing the problem with your manager will be more than worth your while.

Tales from the Queue

Here's how bad a behind-the-queue situation can get for a programmer: I spent several miserable months at the office of a client who had a very slow and overburdened computer. The company's programmers and production users shared the computer resources, but priority was given to the production jobs. Often, the programmers—who arrived at 8 a.m.—could not even sign on until midmorning because the production batch nightly job streams weren't completed until then.

Since this was a temporary consulting job, I had to put up with the situation—for a while. But after several months, my frustration about my inability to get the job done was so intense that I simply quit. I went into the owner's office and told him that nobody could do the work he expected to be done without being given the computer time necessary to do it.

I would never have taken a permanent job that required laboring under those conditions. You shouldn't, either. But if you are already working at a company that constricts your chances for success because of wait-time in a queue, it's up to you to speak to your manager about the problem.

Tell your manager how much time you are wasting waiting for your programs to compile. This will probably not be news to him. The company owners have thought about this, and have probably decided they would rather not, say, run production jobs at night (because they'd have to pay for security guards and computer operators at night). So they make production and programming share day computer time. But they will try to remedy the situation only if programmers chafing under restrictive conditions let their managers know how much of their time is being wasted. Programmers are expensive; security guards and operators come cheap. Enlightened managers can eliminate the queues for both production users and programmers, but only if they know about the problems queues cause and understand the overwhelming economic and psychological benefits of getting rid of them.

The Best Compile Strategy

You will quickly realize that when you write and test very large corporate source programs, you must focus primarily on the block of work you just coded or are reviewing, and have confidence that your prior code works and was well tested as you wrote it.

Successful programmers quickly learn to work in very small blocks of code and in small bursts of intensive effort; then they have the computer validate—or invalidate—the last effort and its effect on the entire program. I may compile a program or several programs 100 or more times a day, validating each programming block of work, testing the results of the added code, and building success upon success, until the program is complete enough to be considered unit-tested.

Working on small blocks of programming functions and getting positive reinforcement of your latest effort makes your mind work best, and drives you to keep on. When you use this method, you will consider even complex programs easy. The computer is waiting to compile and validate your latest programming; you need only make use of it. So use the computer all day, every day, as you program.

$$ The Bottom Line $$

Don't take a job at a company that denies you instant access to its computer—meaning instant response to each of your compiles. This access allows you to work in small blocks of code. Validating each programming block of work and testing the results of the added code (thus building success upon success) will make even complex programs seem easy. Sparing the computer the trouble of continual compiling is fatuous. Compile your work 100 times a day, if you must, to get it right as you move along.

Chapter Eleven

Take On the Tough Jobs

To be a successful corporate programmer, you have got to have goals—conscious goals. To be spectacularly successful as a corporate programmer, you also need audacity—the willingness to tackle those high-visibility, risky projects that your colleagues are afraid to touch.

"Imagine how creative this guy is," says programmer/consultant Dennis Mulcare, shaking his head in awe. "Garry's sitting there coding one program with his right hand, coding another program with his left hand, analyzing some other difficult problem in his head, and talking on the phone. There are people in this world who can have four or five thoughts going on in their mind at the same time, and Garry is one of them."

Garry Reinhard is a superb programmer—the most gifted programmer I have ever met. But it wasn't simply his innate talent that shot him to the top; also required was an inexorable drive toward his goals and the supreme self-confidence that allowed him to achieve those goals.

Very few programmers have Garry's innate ability. But even if your talents are far more modest than his, you can become a highly paid corporate programmer—as long as (a) your goal is to become one, (b) you have Garry's formidable drive and readiness to keep on learning, and (c) you're willing, as Garry was always willing, to take on the high-visibility projects that your colleagues consider too daunting.

Garry has gone from computer operator to audacious IBM systems engineer to co-developer of a breakthrough software package to ownership of his own firm. Telling Garry's story is, I believe, the best way to illustrate this chapter's theme: setting goals and not being afraid to take risks.

"I Had a Dream—to Get Ahead"

I met Garry more than thirty years ago, when I was a systems engineer at IBM. I was giving a course in System/360 RPG for programmers new to the IBM System/360 computer. Garry was an eighteen-year-old programmer who was taking the class because his company was switching from the older and smaller 1440 computer. To give my students a little rest and recreation, I had them take what I call the Twelve Balls Test, a notoriously difficult logic test. Garry was the only one in the class who came up with the solution.

(Can you, too, find the solution? Technical interviewers giving in-depth evaluations have used this test for many years to judge whether job applicants think logically. It's a killer. I've rarely found anyone who can solve it without hours and hours of trial and error. If you'd like to take the test, go to my Web site, *www.harkinsaudit.com/logictest*. You'll find the test, and some hints on how to proceed, there.)

Like most of us first- and second-generation computer-language programmers, Garry learned by chance about the field for which his brain and temperament seem to have been specially calibrated. When he was in high school, programming wasn't a likely goal for anyone.

"Back then, if you looked up 'Programmers' in the want ads, you found ads for the people who scheduled programming on radio stations," he says. But, he points out, *"I always had a dream—to get ahead."* Even then, Gary knew the power of having a specific goal.

To be a successful corporate programmer, you have got to have goals—conscious and documented goals. Maybe your immediate goal is to move up to the next job title in two years, or to move from programming maintenance to new application development, or to get assigned to a high-visibility project. Maybe your immediate goal is to learn a hot new programming language, or to develop an in-house standards manual, or to continue professional education. Maybe you recognize a need for finding a valued mentor, or learning an important and widely used software package, or keenly observing how the top programmers and consultants work. Your goals, whatever they are, they should be always be at the back of your mind. And writing your goals down on paper (I do this) will add to your motivation and to your success.

Driving Toward the Goal

As I got to know Garry (who worked with me at IBM and also as a co-developer of a software package), the knowledge that he had been an Eagle Scout quickly clued me in that he was a high achiever. (Only 4 percent of Boy Scouts become Eagle Scouts.) The capacity to work on tough projects and see them through as an adult is a predictable consequence of setting high goals for yourself when you're young.

Garry is the programmer I have in mind when I encourage people without a college education to go into this field. He became a top programmer even though he had only five months of formal education beyond high school. (Garry got into programming at the dawn of the IT age. I acknowledge that it may be tougher, in the new millennium, to start out in programming without a degree. Still, it can be done. According to the federal Bureau of Labor Statistics, 3 out of 5 programmers had a bachelor's degree or higher in 2,000—but 12 percent had only a high-school education or less, and another 17 percent had, like Garry, "some college, no degree.")

It was those classic precursors of success—native talent, ambition, the willingness to work hard, and opportunity—that shot Garry to the top and kept him there.

> *Two years before he graduated from high school, Garry worked three nights a week at a retail outlet packing Christmas toys. "My boss liked me," he says. "He asked if I wanted to be a regular part-time worker. 'We've got two job openings,' he said. 'One's in accounting, one's in data processing.' I gave him a dumb look. I didn't know anything about either one. So he took me to the accounting department. There were maybe 500 people in there with white shirts and ties. Nobody's communicating. It was like walking into a room with 500*

corpses; they just looked up and followed us with their eyes. I said, 'This looks boring as hell to me.'

"Next thing I know, we go into this room where you need to have a pass code. The door opens and on the left side there's a glass wall in front of all these computers. A guy comes out with a suit on and my boss says, 'This is our head programmer.' The guy in the suit turns to me and says, 'When are you going to come work with us and be a programmer like me? You get to wear a suit all the time and act like a jerk.' The other guys in the department say to me, 'We need some young blood. Come work with us.' The whole personality of everybody in there was different. I said, 'This is where I want to work. Right here.'"

When Garry graduated from high school, the company wouldn't let him do shift work after 11 p.m.; he was, they said, too young. So, while working part time, he went to a school in Philadelphia that taught programming.

"I got into a class with five people and a wonderful teacher who actually programmed for a living," he says. "I was the kid in the class. I attended school for five months—during which I got two months of training on the tabulating machine [this is the machine that had been invented by Hermann Hollerith for the 1890 census]. School was very hard. While I was taking these classes I started working as a computer operator at a company that made bridal gowns.

"I was the worst computer operator ever. I had started writing programs to make my operator job easier. Finally they told me they were either going to fire me or make me a programmer trainee. That's how I went from operator to programmer."

The way up required massive doses of new information, and Garry taught himself because he knew what he wanted. To program the new IBM System/360, he had to learn RPG. By reading a book, he learned the original RPG. Then, just by reading more books, he taught himself IBM's Assembler language, than RPG II and PL/I.

"Programming also involved learning different operating systems, communication systems, and how they interact. I dealt with IBM's DOS for the System/360, OS, MVS, MTCS, and CICS, among others, all of which I learned on the job.

"I worked like a dog seven days a week—till four in the morning and on Saturdays and Sundays. I didn't care. It was important to learn my trade. The job interested me, I liked it, and I wanted to get good at it."

Risking Failure in Full View

Later, Garry went to work as a systems engineer for IBM. When other, more experienced programmers would demur about taking on some complex project, Garry would ask for the job. Then he'd analyze intricate problems, find innovative solutions, and write elegant code, with amazing speed and accuracy, in IBM's difficult CICS macro level Assembler language.

Garry's willingness to take on the high-visibility, difficult projects that his colleagues shunned would eventually be significantly—indeed, spectacularly—rewarded.

"IBM hired me because I could do things," Garry acknowledges. "They stuck me on projects that other people couldn't do or didn't want to do. I wasn't afraid. I'd try anything. It didn't matter how hard a problem it was, or how big—I'd work at it till I got it.

"For instance, no other programmer at IBM wanted to take on the job of winning the Atlantic City casino business. Whoever automated the casinos would have to devise a hotel system, a casino system, and a cash register system that could handle room, credit card, comp (free), and city ledger (house charge) accounts. They wanted a system that completely integrated their hotel, casino, and food and beverage operations.

"Now, IBM did not have a cash register that would work on a System/3, model 15D, computer. My partner, Jim Elias, and I decided on using IBM banking terminals and adding on cash drawers. (I had never before worked in the retail-food/beverage industry, let alone used bank terminals to handle the requirements of these industries.)

"The code was written in Assembler language on punched cards. Each week for eight weeks, Jim and I would fly from Philadelphia to Boca Raton to compile or test our program through a big mainframe computer at a remote site in Palo Alto. No one in IBM banking had ever used the disk controller we were attempting to use.

"We used equipment that had never been used before and adapted it into technologies that it had never been used for before. We had only six months to do it, and IBM didn't think we could. It was a risk; it put our reputation on the line and IBM's reputation on the line. But I knew we could do it. If you can program a computer to do what you want it to do, you can make it do anything.

"We got the project completed in time for the opening of Resorts International Casino. The result was that IBM landed a huge amount of unanticipated business."

IBM was dramatically—flamboyantly—grateful. How tough a job was it? Tough enough to justify Garry's nomination not merely for an Eagle award ($5,000 cash in a briefcase) but a double Eagle ($10,000).

And the presentation! "They awarded it at an afternoon sales conference in Veterans Stadium," Garry says. "Five other guys, from other places in the region, also got Eagles that day—but not double Eagles."

So there he was, lined up in the tunnel at Veterans Stadium with the other winners, wearing a Philadelphia Eagles jacket. When they flashed his photograph on the scoreboard and called out his name, he trotted out of the tunnel to the rah-rahs of the crowd, shook the hand of the president and vice-president of the division, accepted the suitcase with the money, then stood in line with the other winners "the way the football players do, waiting for the next name to be called."

That must have been one challenging project.

The Ultimate Goal: Founding Your Own Firm

The ultimate goal of some corporate programmers is independence—first, perhaps, as a consultant and then as the founder of a firm. "You have to look ahead and have good timing," Garry says. "Let's say there were ten steps to where I am now. Between every step there were fifteen alternative avenues. I never took them, for whatever reason. For instance, I could have been an IT director, but I chose not to—and I'm glad I didn't."

Garry relishes the independence he achieved by founding his own firm. "If you work all the time as an employee at a single company and you don't like those people, you have to leave the company to get away from them. But in our software development and support business, I might spend three days a week at a client, perhaps eight times a year, and I don't have to deal with them any more than that.

"If a customer is really unreasonable and difficult, I tell him, 'Why don't you people go away?' Then they get scared that they won't have any support." That's what you can do when you own your own firm.

"But risks come with the independence. Let's say our client has a $200-million business and wants a new warehouse distribution system. You do the warehousing design. But what happens if doesn't work smoothly and they can't ship for three weeks? That's a big risk. A consultant is always at a high level of exposure. But when you're successful, you're exhilarated—it feels great."

$$ The Bottom Line $$

You don't need coding genius to become a successful (highly paid) programmer. You must, however, have a clear goal that is vital to you, the willingness to devote fierce focus and long hours to getting there, the self-confidence to know when you're ready for the tough jobs, and the courage to take them on.

CHAPTER TWELVE

Mission: Impossible

With risk comes stress—stress that can be nearly intolerable. How bad can the stress get, and what can a programmer do to mitigate it? This chapter tells the story of a "Mission: Impossible" scenario that ended giving this consulting programmer a career boost.

The programmer who will become really successful is the programmer who reaches out and embraces ever more challenging, high-visibility projects—even those that come with the unknowns that signify risk. He or she never stops learning, never stops searching for something more.

With risk, however, comes stress—stress that can be nearly intolerable. How bad can the stress get, and what can a programmer do to mitigate it? This chapter tells the story of a "Mission: Impossible" scenario that ended giving this consulting programmer a career boost.

Life on the Road for a Consulting Programmer

One weekday night about seven o'clock, while I was (of course) still working my normal ten-hour billable day at my client's office, I got a phone call.

It was safe to talk because my cube mate had already gone home—as had the other programmers in the surrounding cubes that were within hearing. The call was from a trusted business associate, who was offering me the possibility of a new consulting job. He said the job was a mere 60 or so miles away from my home, so I could commute to work rather than staying in a motel (as I was presently doing), that it paid more, and it was a long-term gig. It was very exciting work, he said, and the people were very nice, I would have a private office, and he was sure that, with my unbelievable skills and experience, I could handle it.

He was just a little vague about exactly what the consulting job entailed, but he said they really needed a person of my caliber right away, and did I want to start as soon as I could extricate myself from my current client? Ignoring the signals he was sending about how tough the job was, I said "Yes."

So I bade fond farewell to the beautiful babbling waterfall in the lobby in the client's modern building and to my buddies and headed for my new exciting opportunity, anticipating soundly sleeping at home every work night. I was to sleep at home every night, but not exactly very soundly for some time.

First Morning—So Far, So Good

After quite a few years and many jobs, you get a pretty good feel about a place on your first day. This job started off terrific.

There was plenty of free parking in the company parking lot, and my programming manager welcomed me warmly and escorted me to my large and very well equipped private office. My office was near the coffee area, where the company provided free coffee, tea, hot chocolate, and bottled spring water for our convenience.

My new manager introduced me to my programming peers (who all smiled) and to the other managers in the IT department and spent considerable time reviewing my job responsibilities. I was now responsible for the support and enhancement of a comprehensive warehouse distribution Radio Frequency (RF) bar-coding system, where hundreds of packers in warehouses scan bar-coded items into cartons for shipment to major retail chains nationwide. That seemed to be an exciting and interesting application, especially since I had never worked on that specific application before. I did a little quick math (division) and estimated that the company packed and shipped about $1 million of goods every hour of every working day.

My programming manager said that he was really glad that I was there because they were having some trouble keeping the system running smoothly, and that they had many required enhancements that had to be put into the system to keep up with constantly changing customer shipping compliance issues.

Dawning Dismay

I inquired what happened when there was trouble with the system. He answered that either the packers couldn't scan the bar-coded tickets into the cartons or the cartons would be packed incorrectly. That could cause customer shipment deadlines to be missed, trucks missing scheduled deliveries, and customer returns or charge-backs (credits). As I began to sense how high-visibility and high-risk a job this was, I inquired how big the charge-backs might be. As I recall, he said, "As much as $50,000 per shipment."

For some reason, my hands started to get a little sweaty, so I asked who would train me in this job and perhaps temporarily share responsibility for support of this critical business function. My manager smiled and told me that I had come with this terrific reputation, and that I would have to tackle this one on my own.

Then I asked how often there were problems with the system, and he said, "Quite often." By now, I had my handkerchief out and my eyes on the door, but then I thought about those nights in the motel and that I had left a job to take this one, and I determined to at least make it through the first day.

Probing a little further, I asked for the comprehensive application documentation for this critical RF business function, thinking that I could quickly get an overview of this apparently very comprehensive and heavily modified warehouse distribution software package. My manager smiled and told me that because of the very extensive in-house modifications made to the package of several millions of lines of source code, there really was no comprehensive application documentation. He suggested that I learn the system by reviewing the source code in the Radio Frequency bar-code scanning program, which

controlled how the hundreds of warehouse packers scanned the
bar-coded items into cartons based on customer orders for shipment.

I got myself a cup of coffee and settled into my quiet private office
to (I hoped) quickly learn this new system by reviewing the big RF
scanning program. Just how big that first program was became appar-
ent when I utilized the computer source editor to review the program.
This allowed me to look at seventeen lines of the source program at a
time on my nice, large-screen PC. I scanned for the bottom of the
source program and saw that there were some 7,600 source statements in the program, which meant that there were 447 pages of
source code for me to review on the screen, and this did not include externally described files and copybook expanded statements.

So I decided to compile the source program and review the compile
listing, which would include the externally described files and the expanded copybook statements. The compile listing was 300 pages long,
and there were 11,500 source statements in the compile listing, including the expanded externally described and copybook expanded
source statements.

I then wondered if this software package utilized program call
statements to access other programs, which would perform part of the
processing logic for this program. Some software packages break the
application logic into many sub-programs, while other software packages put virtually all of the program logic into one "pleasingly plump"
program. I scanned for the CALL operation, and was surprised to find
36 CALL statements to other programs from this program. That meant
that I had to review 36 more programs to understand and support this
one RF scanning program. I then reviewed the several dozen disk files
that were input and output to the program, and found that, of course,
I wasn't familiar with any of them.

To put this in perspective, one of the key programs that I had to
support in my new company was about the size of this book, and it referenced 36 other programs during its program execution, and I had
not worked on this vendor's software package before. I had better get
busy before something happened, and we couldn't pack and ship.

I had just gotten my second cup of coffee and flipped open the 300-page compile listing of the RF bar-code scanning program when my manager knocked on my door.

He was not smiling, and in fact he seemed a little excited. Something had happened, and hundreds of packers were not packing, and cartons were not flowing along the conveyors, and trucks would be arriving, and customer shipments could be missed, and there would be big charge-backs.

He asked if I, his new programmer with the stellar reputation, knew how to fix it, and I had to gently tell him I hadn't even known anything was wrong—the phone had rung in his office, and apparently in his manager's office.

To his credit, my manager didn't ask me how long it would take to fix it, because by now he knew better than to ask that question. We both sat down to figure out logically what had caused the problem in this really incredibly complex real-time environment, in warehouses that were hundreds of miles away.

At that point, though I am generally opposed to guessing, I did use some of my trouble-shooting experience to root around and guess what might be wrong. Having no other possible solution, we tried my guess, and by gosh, it worked. Now I was the real expert, and I had narrowly escaped being well known (but not admired) by management of the company on my first day. I hate to guess about a critical programming problem, because that often leads to a series of wilder and wilder guesses, lost time and focus, and, ultimately, disaster. But in this one case I had no choice.

How to Master a Killer Project

Though this first crisis was over, I was actually terrified at being so responsible for a critical business function and being so unprepared for it. I resolved to master this program and the entire millions of lines of code that it encompassed. I could not do that, however, without first mastering the business function—the warehouse system—itself.

My manager took me to a local warehouse and walked me through every stage of the customer order being picked, bar-code scanned, and packed into cartons. By seeing the actual business function being performed, I could much more easily visualize what the computer programs that automated the function should do. Then the many programs that I had to learn, support, and enhance made much more sense to me, as they were simply the procedures that some programmer had automated as source text in a computer program rather than in a procedures manual.

I learned the warehouse business function by watching a single packer scanning items into a carton, much the way a supermarket cashier scans and packs groceries. What I couldn't see or visualize was all the detailed information generated by the hundreds of other packers in warehouses far remote from the IT department. In a warehouse environment there are crisis-creating events that not even a good project design can anticipate—scanner, scale, or conveyor problems; power outages; inaccurate labeling; poor bar-code quality. And, of course, human frailty: trainee packers getting the job done in ways no programmer could anticipate; packers abandoning their unpacked carton after getting a phone call. Unexpected warehouse events that could potentially cause problems show that new issues can occur months and years after a system is implemented, and are missed in even a good project design.

I worked hard at being able to see exactly what every packer did, including every pick-ticket he worked on, every item he scanned, and every mistake he made, and exactly when he made it. I kept track of details by putting in "Hello" statements for everything that happened in that RF scanning program, and then in virtually every other complex program that I had to understand, support, and enhance. I couldn't hear what the packers said when they got those phone calls, but everything they did in the packing process was mine to see and master.

It all ended well.

$$ The Bottom Line $$

There's not much you can do prevent experiencing major stress in an intensely focused, high-responsibility, high-pressure job. So you soldier on—with medication, meditation, or, when you get home, the blood-pressure-lowering benefits of long sessions in an easy chair with the cat on your lap. Comfort yourself with the knowledge that stress produces adrenalin, and adrenaline can galvanize you into action that boosts your career.

CHAPTER THIRTEEN

How Your Work Is Tracked

*You are the very visible author of your programs. All of your work
in every program is testimony to your skill or lack of skill.*

In the real world of corporate programming, the programmer is often
the project manager of his own programming projects. Indeed, only
projects that involve several programmers are normally assigned a project manager, whose primary responsibility is to coordinate the activities
of the programmers. Whether your project has a project manager or you
are your own project manager, you need to be familiar with how a project lands on your desk so that you can shine at every opportunity.

How a Project Usually Starts

The IT programming manager normally receives requests for programming projects from managers of end user departments. Typically, a
manager is dealing with a large backlog of user or mandated requests
for programming work; he needs to record, prioritize, and acknowledge
the requests before attempting to assign them to programmers.

When a project is a go, the IT programming manager forwards the
approved request to a programmer with the project documentation
and authorization, with a note "(please) do it." At least for small projects, the programmer is then totally responsible for assigning the project number—normally through a project change management system—and then designing, coding, testing, and documenting the project
before turning the completed project over for final review and implementation. Any programmer questions about the project should be
handled in the programmer's daily one-minute review with his or her

manager or the programmer's weekly summary report to the manager (or clarification with the manager, as needed).

Every programming manager makes some kind of estimate of the time it should take to complete a project, even if he doesn't tell the programmer what that estimate is. The estimate will vary according to the skill of the programmer—sometimes by a factor of five for the same project, depending on the programmer's previously demonstrated performance. The estimated project time and the actual project time will vary according to the programmer's skill, the productivity tools utilized, and the manager's ability to communicate the project requirements; the time and effort the manager puts into reviewing the progress of the project; and the time spent in testing, final project review and turnover of the project.

Of course, your manager will probably ask you for some kind of rough estimate of the completion date of the project; for large or critical projects you may be asked for rough estimates of the time it will take to reach various checkpoints. My advice on giving estimated completion dates is to be honest (not too optimistic) and give the date by which you think you can produce a quality product.

What the Project Number Means to Your Career

A project number or project code is usually assigned to even the smallest or most mundane programming change. It is definitely assigned to new requests, new programs, and all complex programming activity—even activity internal to the IT department. Along with the project number will be your name.

The project number allows for detailed reporting, management, and analysis of simple to complex and expensive programming activity using a variety of project management software tools. Savvy IT managers use a wealth of project information to track not only the progress of the project but to compare the actual costs to budgeted or projected costs, as well as to track programmer productivity and performance. If you slack off and that time ends up recorded under a particular project number, don't be surprised if it comes back to you in a very bad way.

Projects and Project Numbers Can Live Forever

Every change or new program is put into production by the project number—that is, at least in companies utilizing programming change management programs to manage changes to their computer production programs.

You are the very visible author of your programs. All of your work in every program is testimony to your skill or lack of skill.

So you are known by your programming projects, including their number, size, and complexity and their success or failure. Your programming manager should be using the results of your work on your programming projects as an objective measurement of your productivity and performance—and, probably, your ability and your value to the company.

Some of my programs have run in production for twenty-five years, and I routinely work on programs that have run that long. After a while you can predict the quality of a programming change, even one made twenty-five years ago, by looking at the programmer's name in the source program project change information. Pride in your work is yet another reason to do high-quality and readable programming: Your name is on it.

$$ The Bottom Line $$

Almost everything relating to programming is defined and measured as a project. Sometimes, even the programmer himself is considered a project, or a project-in-process, in the sense that he is in need of polishing his skills, or his attitude, or his productivity.

CHAPTER FOURTEEN

Boost Your Output and
Lower Your Stress with Productivity Tools

Highly successful programmers don't work any harder than average programmers: They just work smarter and faster.

Y ou have the power to more than double your programming productivity on the job—right now—if only you'll wield it. This chapter will teach you how.

Why Are Some Programmers So Productive?

Highly successful programmers don't work any harder than average programmers: They just work smarter and faster. They set out to understand how their client's business works—to master the flow of production from one department to the next. They continually hone their coding skills, consciously aiming at writing simple and efficient (and therefore elegant) code. And—just as important—they boost their output by searching out, and asking their manager to provide them with, the powerful hardware and software corporate programming productivity tools that are on the market.

I find it mystifying that the use of productivity tools is such a minority practice in the hundreds of IT shops in which I have worked or consulted. I've observed, over and over, that only a few programmers in any information technology department bother to take advantage of these brain-multipliers. Most of the programmers I see in action don't use, and certainly don't ask for, proven productivity tools that would multiply their performance.

Why is that? My conclusion, after forty years of observing thousands of programmers in action, is that a programmer's pride in his own brainpower is (ironically) what sometimes keeps him from using his brain. Evidently, most corporate programmers have convinced themselves that they can solve even byzantine programming problems without the help of anyone, thank you—and, most particularly, without the help of the computer itself.

Racing Computer, Plodding Programmer

When I was a systems engineer at IBM, our corporate executive consultant to the apparel industry used to give management seminars to corporate CEOs around the world. As he discussed future economic and computer directions and corporate strategy, he'd refer to a chart that showed "hardware performance" increasing dramatically over time, but the line for "programmer productivity" staying flat.

That chart was presented twenty-five years ago, but it's still valid. Today, computer hardware is thousands of times more powerful than it was back then, but programmers today are only marginally better than they used to be—unless they use productivity tools. The programmer's brain today is essentially what it was twenty-five years ago, and no doubt it will be the same twenty-five years from now. It is the power of the computer itself—which allows techniques like prototyping programs and the use of powerful software productivity tools—that makes the programmer who uses these techniques and tools so much smarter than his peers and his predecessors.

No programmer is talented enough to spurn the productivity tools of his trade. I know that I am not, even though I'm a top-level consulting programmer. Indeed, I probably need the help of productivity tools even more acutely than a journeyman programmer does, since I'm the one who's called in at crisis time—like when a company's warehouse system is threatening to collapse. As a disaster-prevention programmer, I've learned to embrace any productivity tool that can help me fix a system before it explodes.

Specific Productivity Tools and Their Value to You

This is a partial list of important corporate programmer productivity tools that I consider necessary to boost my output and lower my stress when I'm dealing with difficult work.

I've noted down an estimate of the value of each of these tools, based on my forty years' experience working both with and without each of these tools. The "plus" percentage I've listed is the productivity advantage I believe programmers enjoy if they have this tool; the "minus" percentage represents the productivity disadvantage they labor under if they do not have this tool. The increase or decrease in productivity refers to both the speed of completion of the delivered programming project and its quality. I have purposely left out of this analysis the differing effects of a good manager versus a bad manager on a programmer's productivity.

Programmer Working Environment and Project Management

- Very fast and always available corporate computer
  Plus 75%, minus 50%

  There is no excuse for your company not to give you the tools you need. If you have mediocre tools, you will be a mediocre producer. There is no other way to put it.

- Private, quiet programming environment
  Plus 25%, minus 25%

  A private office may not be a reality for some programmers today, but it is a reality for others—and a reality you should make one of your goals.

- High-quality project specifications and project management
  Plus 75%, minus 75%

  Without a roadmap and a destination, your project is doomed to failure. Make sure you get the information you need to start and finish your project.

- Full testing environment with representative data
  Plus 30%, minus 30%

  Testing is the sign of a professional programmer. If you don't
  test and your program crashes spectacularly, you can't offer up
  as a consolation prize the fact that you saved time and money by
  not testing your work.

- Comprehensive continuing education and reference material
  Plus 20%, minus 30%

  This includes an in-house IT reference library of appropriate
  manuals, magazines, and books purchased by your employer.

Programmer Software Productivity Tools

- Comprehensive program logic and data auditing tool
  Plus 30%, minus 40%

  Program logic and data auditing tools are critical to programming success, because they provide at least a glimpse of what is
  happening inside the computer as your program is executing. At
  best they allow you to see the panorama of what is happening
  inside your program. There are program steppers that allow
  stopping the program at a specific statement as it is executed,
  and there are program auditors that record all the statements
  as they execute, with the data processed on disk for review. You,
  too, can create a program auditing capability that will enable
  you to see exactly what is happening inside the computer as
  your program executes, including the source statements as they
  execute and the data as it is processed by complex computer
  code. I consider this auditing (or visualization) capability of the
  program and data to be the capability most useful to programmers attempting to master a program fat with complicated code.

- Disk File Utility (to display and change disk records)
  Plus 15%, minus 15%

A disk file utility program allows the programmer to select, display, change, add, and delete disk file records, and to change the contents of the fields on the disk record. This is a powerful and much-needed programmer productivity tool. I've found the most important advantage of a disk file utility tool to be that it allows me to visualize all of the information in an entire disk record or group of records. I can see the field descriptions and the data in each field in the record, and it is easy to see the related information for, say, a customer in the record that contains the customer master information. Just looking at the information the company keeps on a master file disk record for customers, products, orders, or inventory enables me to quickly associate the actual customer data (such as ABC Company) with the field name that is used in the programs to access this information, like CUNAME.

The first thing I do as a programmer trying to understand a complex program that uses files that I do not know is to print the program compile listing and hand-write the file description next to the file name— for instance, for file CUSTP I would write "Customer Master File by Customer Number." I then use the disk file utility productivity tool to (1) display a customer master record and visualize the data fields in that customer master record, and (2) relate them to record field names. In my own programs I enter the file description and the access path (key sequence) as a comment for each of the files used in my program. I do this to visualize in my mind the file and its key—and indeed the fields in the file as I start the program—and also as a courtesy for me and for others who will follow.

- Structured Query Language (SQL) or Query

Plus 15%, minus 15%

A Structured Query Language utility provides the programmer with a very widely utilized method of querying, updating, inserting, and deleting disk file records with easy-to-use commands like SELECT, INSERT, DELETE.

Programmers without this SQL program or the disk file utility program would have to write programs frequently to do these functions (which are needed daily in a programming environment), taking time and incurring risks that these quickie programs are not correct. A programmer virtually always needs to create or modify and then review test data so that program testing is comprehensive. However, in my opinion, that does not provide the wonderful visualization capability that is provided by a disk file utility program.

- Comprehensive project (program) change management system
  Plus 20%, minus 25%

  A project, or program, change management system is a software utility that automates and documents the implementation of projects into the company's development and production environments. It also archives the previous source programs and executable object programs being replaced. This allows a history to be kept of that previous production level, and it allows for back-out of the programming change and recovery of the previous level, if that becomes necessary. Every corporate computing department has some change management procedure, even if it is manual and undocumented, to implement programming changes. Automated and comprehensive project change management systems greatly smooth and simplify the project implementation process.

- Comprehensive file, field and program cross-reference tool
  Plus 10%, minus 10%

  There are comprehensive software utility programs that provide cross-references among programs, files, and fields. These cross-references are normally created by major business function or application software packages, so programmers working in that area, such as financial, customer relationship management (CRM), manufacturing, or distribution, can quickly reference all the program-related information—often tens of thousands of fields, records, files, and programs—when that information is needed.

Getting the Tools You Need

There are dozens—perhaps hundreds—of other tools that can enhance the programmer's capability and give him the power to master programs he could never otherwise complete. It is human nature (at least, mine) to try almost infinitely hard to succeed at something important. But even a programming bulldog will eventually give up when constantly stymied.

The question is, can you get the tools you need? Some tools (like a private office and a fast computer) are assets you know you will have or not have before you take a programming job. You will have to inform yourself about the other productivity tools available to you.

Unfortunately, many managers don't understand their programmers' need for productivity tools—particularly software productivity tools. They may lack this savvy because they never did programming work, or they did their programming before the advent of these powerful tools, and before the rise of the networked and mission-critical environment common in today's corporate computing. All too often I have heard a manager say, "Why do you need that?" or "First time I heard of that" when a programmer requests a widely known and reviewed productivity tool.

So it will probably be up to you to make a clear case for your manager's getting that tool. To explain why you need it and how it will increase your output—even to find out that such a tool is available—you'll need to keep up on developments in your field. But that's no burden. In fact, you are probably on various mailing lists that bring you, unbidden, IT newsletters chockablock with new-product evaluations and suggestions for free educational downloads. For the sake of your career you need to keep networking, going to users' conferences, scanning technical Websites like mcpressonline.com and ibm.com, and buying and reading books and magazines aimed at programmers. When you learn about a new tool you think might help you in your work, clip the product review and have it handy to show your manager.

Your company's information technology department budget will typically be about 1 percent of the gross sales of the company, depending on the industry and the individual company. As the hardware continually drops in price, the majority of the costs are in personnel, including programmers. Spending just 1 percent of that budget on productivity tools and professional development for its programmers would generate a burst of productivity by addressing the greatest barrier to dynamism in an IT department—the human-neuron-bound, plodding pace of its programmers.

You, like your IT department, should be willing to spend 1 percent of your annual salary on your own independent professional development—programming books, programming magazines, and professional seminars and off-site meetings. Many corporate programmers do not spend any of their personal time or money on their own professional development, and they don't press their IT management for continuing professional development and productivity tools. And they and their company suffer for it.

$$ The Bottom Line $$

It is easy to become complacent on the job; too many programmers do just that. To be less vulnerable to downsizing and more eligible for promotion, you need to become one of the best programmers in your department. But you won't outstrip your colleagues by arrogantly deciding to use your brainpower alone. Start calling on the power of productivity tools.

CHAPTER FIFTEEN

A Blueprint for Savvy Programming

*A user for whom you are designing a system can be your best advo-
cate or your worst nightmare. Even difficult or reluctant users can
be brought around if the programmer is courteous and respectful.
Determining the end user's needs, along with the project specs, is
the first step in this five-step blueprint for savvy programming.*

One of the ways you can prove yourself valuable to your company
and to your manager is to be able to take on tasks beyond coding.
Most programmers can take well-written specifications from a manager or a systems analyst and write code to match those specifications.
The next step beyond being simply a journeyman programmer is to become good at developing specifications from user and management input. In this chapter, I'll go through the steps you must master before
you're ready to advance in your career.

Step 1: Get the Project Specifications

If you usually get your specifications from your manager or a systems analyst, going to the end user may be a big step for you, but it's
an important skill to learn. When there's no systems analyst on the
project, you will have to go directly to the user and get the specs, normally starting with the output report or desired screen or function
that the user wants. Then you work that back through the input that's
required—perhaps disk files, or whatever—and then the data that the
user might have to enter online.

You gather all this into programming specifications—either for a new program (perhaps a new application or a new online function) or for the maintenance of an existing function.

Sound easy? It isn't too difficult if you have a user who is able to clearly identify and communicate his requirements. But that is not always the case. After you've worked with a user for a while, you'll be able to gauge the quality of his requests—which are savvy, which are not well thought out, which are frivolous. You'll know, with experience, which users have done their homework and focused intelligently on the problem. It's a pleasure to work with savvy users. But you must be able to work with all users, and it is your job to lead them to the correct solution. You cannot let the user dominate in IT areas in which you are more qualified than he is.

So you must take the user's request, clarify it, and try to understand it. Then you should go back to the user and have a dialog to make sure that his request is legitimate, that you can do it, that the results will be satisfactory to the user. Your job is to "see through" the user's request, to focus on what the real problem is, to come up with the correct solution to that problem, and to lead the user to accept your definition of the proper solution.

The more savvy and experienced a programmer is, the fewer specs he needs, but if the request is for a change to an existing display screen or printed report, I expect a picture of the screen or report with the requested changes clearly identified. Printers have always insisted on specific, numbered changes to a business form, for very good reason—because that is the only clear way to identify and freeze the changes. After you've done similar programming functions, and when you have enough experience to understand the business functions or applications, you won't need much in terms of formal specs. You might need only a sketch of the newly requested output or a conversation with an end user to determine readily a very good way to do that application.

If the request is for a core business function that you already know, you can be very helpful to the end user in refining his request. Indeed, you can fill in the details and come up with a much more elegant and useful function than most users could dream of. Once you've done that, the user will learn to rely on your work and request that you do more work for him.

Step 2: Design the Solution to the Request

Having clarified what the user wants, you then ponder the general way to approach the task, using whatever standards the information technology department has set. You then consider how you can get the job done most productively (most quickly and professionally, and with the highest possible quality) in order to improve your company's bottom line.

You can look at similar programs that could be copied. Start with the outputs—the required functions—the inputs, disk files, user data, and any other inputs are then defined and documented. Then the logic of the reports is made final to make sure that that's what the user wants.

This is a good time to go back to the user again, to make sure your preliminary understanding of what the user wants is correct. If you are working with a new concept, a new application like online order entry, or something that affects many users, you would actually do a skeleton (prototype) program. Your skeleton program shows the user the screens in the anticipated flow of end user processing that he will see when the project is in production (without all the logic, validity checking, and all the other things that are going to be needed in production). Then the user can determine whether you're on the right track. A project prototype is like a movie preview in that it illustrates only the important concepts and functions without the cluttering details required for full implementation.

Let's look at an example: A very, very large company in the apparel field was going from a manual order entry to a real-time online system. In the system to be replaced, the customer service agents were using paper (nine forms!) to record orders, and thirty copies of an inventory availability report that was valid only at 8 o'clock in the morning. Under the new system, they would be relying totally on what they saw in the computer to give information and record orders.

There were some thirty customer service agents involved, dealing with customers around the country and around the world. Making this change would have a huge impact on the owner's system. He knew he needed it; he wanted it; he demanded it (after all, his agents were so bogged down in paperwork that sometimes they had to let the phone ring *for twenty minutes* before answering it). That meant that every day, customers who were ready to order became impatient and offended, hung up, and probably went elsewhere. But the senior vice-president in charge of order-entry customer service was very apprehensive about the changeover to a real-time online system. If the new system had glitches, he told the owner, it could actually destroy the company. At the very least, if it didn't work, it would create an enormous problem.

Under the owner's direction, I designed the system. We made a skeleton demonstration for the senior vice-president. He came in, looked at it, and went through the typical order-booking scenarios, doing all the variations that the agents would have to do. After a fifteen-minute presentation, he said, "Great job. It will absolutely work, and I'm satisfied." The rest of the job was simply filling in the production details, like checking product availability dates and getting input on specific needs and desires from the customer-service manager, the vice-president, and the company president. Proceeding so cautiously, and keeping the users part of the process, guaranteed that the installation would be a huge success. And it was. Every agent was able to answer the phone *on the first ring*, and the inventory they were promising was actually still available when they promised it.

That illustrates the way to turn a skeptic—indeed, someone whose job depends on the success of an application—into an active proponent of your efforts. Once you get the person in charge behind you, all the other people in that department will fall into line.

It is important to note here that the user for whom you are designing a system can be your best advocate or your worst nightmare. Even difficult or reluctant users can be brought around if the programmer is

courteous and respectful. Ask questions and then listen to their requests and suggestions. If users are telling everyone in their department (and perhaps the IT department) how helpful you were and how
happy they are with your work, you can imagine the impact on your
manager. On the other hand, if they tell your manager they never
want to see you in their department again...

Step 3: Develop the Project into Blocks of Work

When you've determined the specifications, and perhaps done a
prototype program for the user, you can break the application down
into all the steps necessary to accomplish that job.

For instance, printing a report of a sales analysis might be broken
down into three programs: a requestor program, a selection program
to retrieve the requested database information, and a print program to
actually print the report.

These three steps constitute a typical request/extract and a sum-
mary-report print. The output report could also be a display screen as
well as a printed report. That's a typical end user request and application—breaking an end user report into three steps that would be required in terms of programs. A typical company will have hundreds of
these request/extract/print applications to service the information
needs of its many end users.

Step 4: Write the Project Program as a Prototype Program

When you get to the third step in this process of summarizing and
formatting and printing the report to the user's requirements, your
print program may ultimately turn out to be 2,000 or 3,000 program
source statements long when it is put into production.

What I almost always do when doing this kind of project is find an
existing production request/extract/print set of programs for the same
end user department and copy it to my development library, renaming
the programs to those of my project. I then strip out the extraneous
code from the other application and test the prototype (skeleton)

program stream to see if it displays the requestor screen, accepts it, and passes control to the selection and print programs. I am happy if my first print output is the expected report headings.

Then I add in the specific program source code for this project, testing as each block of logic is added to the prototype's program stream—and presto, the whole thing usually works very quickly.

Writing a prototype program is a very efficient way to attack a project. You write a few lines of code, get a clean compile (meaning that the program works in terms of the syntax of the language), and then you constantly build on that.

What you don't do is write a many-thousand-line program and then throw it into the computer. If you do that, you're likely to come up with hundreds (or thousands) of errors. It's far better to write short and build on success. You put down your fundamental logic, put a little bit into the computer, get a clean compile, and then test that skeleton program. As you go along, you add a few lines or thoughts, a little bit of logic. It's wonderful to be able to demonstrate, over and over, that you're correct.

Step 5: Test Your Program Exhaustively with Valid Corporate Data

As I can't help reiterating (it's crucial!), the single most important factor when you're writing a program is your ability to test again and again and again. The completed program should go through as many stages as a painting that started with many sketches and has many layers of paint underneath the completed picture.

I know of some order-entry-type programs (large programs that affect many people and have many functions) that, believe it or not, have been compiled 1,000 times—maybe 100 times during the initial writing, then hundreds of times as functions were added over the years. So what matters is not how many times you compile (don't be afraid to compile often); what matters is how quickly you can compile as you put these little incremental blocks of code in. The capacity to compile quickly will enhance the elegance, and the success, of your program.

Testing your prototyped request/extract/print program project against valid corporate data is vital to its being successfully implemented in production. I test exhaustively—much more than some other programmers—but normally I have been so productive in the early stages of the project that I can spend considerable time testing. I recommend that you have a full test environment where you can safely test update programs and change database information as you need to without touching the corporate production environment. Programmers who test against corporate production databases will get burned.

And don't be reluctant to enlist the help of the users in your testing. Once you have cleaned up the output so that it looks good and the basic data is on the report (or showing on the screen), take your work to the users. Explain that it is an early test of the system, but you would like their input. Users often will find subtle errors that you would not. And again…this is a good way to make friends with users.

That's how you do it. You do it this way over and over again, with different requests, different kinds of data—sales, inventory, order, customer data—but it's always basically the same thing. When you can do this well, then try move on to more creative and more challenging projects as soon as you can.

$$ The Bottom Line $$

No matter the language or platform, all successful projects follow the steps you just read in this chapter. Don't blow your future or your reputation—be methodical in everything you do.

CHAPTER SIXTEEN

Master Millions of Lines of Complex Code

*If you understand the business functions and the information flow
within a corporate job or corporate department, you will understand the purpose and basic content of all the computer programs
that have been written to support them. But what's the best way to
work with a program fat with thousands of lines of source code?*

You can master existing complex programs—programs with tens of
thousands of lines of source code. All you need to do is adopt the
systematic approach I outline in this chapter, which includes both
walking through the business process and then placing audit statements liberally throughout the code. Doing both successfully will
make you a valuable member of your programming team.

First, Walk Through the Business Process

My approach to mastering millions of lines of code, which is usually written in the primary programming language of the company, is
to start with a business function that I know. This is simple: You probably know many of the essential company business processes from
your personal life or from what you've learned in school or a previous
job. If you've worked in a business and been observant, you understand how a company operates.

When I took over programming responsibility for the support and
enhancement of a huge warehouse distribution packing system, I didn't
need to understand how 400 packers worked; all I had to know was how
a single packer worked. So the systems analyst in charge and I walked
out to a local warehouse and watched a packer barcode-scanning items

into cartons with a radio frequency scanner. There were some more details, but I made sure I understood the business function and some needs that were not being currently addressed by the programs before I even looked at programs or code.

So the very first step you must take is to visualize the business process by actually walking through it. (I mean that you should understand the process so well that you can conjure up in your mind images of employees performing the tasks.) If the application is a very familiar one, such as accounts payable, you probably already know the process from having worked on a similar application. Nevertheless, I still recommend that you take that walk to watch the process in action. You may discover some quirks that you would not have known had you not taken this step.

Don't Just Look at the Source Code

Many corporate programmers never get beyond looking at the source code as their basis of understanding business functions and how programs work. These programmers are, I believe, doomed never to understand vast amounts of important business functions or program code, because it is difficult to learn that way. They can't see the business function because when they are looking at the details in the code, they are looking at details that are rarely, if ever, executed. These programmers typically spend their programming careers bored and unhappy because they are focused on support of a tiny part of the corporate business function.

Once you're sure you understand the basic business process or application flow, you should be able to focus on any part of the process. Each corporate job has a well-defined flow of work (which was, before computers, a paperwork flow of inputs and outputs); each segment of a job also has a well-defined flow. If you understand the business functions and the information flow within a corporate job or corporate department, you will understand the purpose and basic content of all the computer programs that have been written to support them. The programs most often simply automate the manual method of perform-ing the business function.

I almost never try to understand much about a business process or an application by just looking at the source code in the programs that support the applications. There is simply too much arcane detail in the programs to allow me to visualize the application flow—or, for that matter, even the program flow.

A complex program like a radio frequency (barcode-scanning) pro-gram, for example, may have thousands of lines of source code, with routines to handle every possible scanning, packing, or error condi-tion. Before I get too involved in the detail of the individual routines, I want to focus on the program mainline before considering all the ex-ceptions in the program. The basic program flow may be one-third of all the source code, and may not be easily identifiable or isolated from the exception routines, and some of the program routines (or sub-procedures) may no longer be valid because of changes to the data being processed, changed operational procedures, or program enhancements.

The Value of Landmarks

If poring over vast amounts of source code is not the best strategy, then what is?

For many years I put landmarks, or "hello" checkpoints, all through a long or complex program. I called these landmarks the "Harkins Trace"; they output a trace of all audited statements and the data being processed to disk for my analysis.

I reasoned that if the traditional memory dump that was caused by a program's abnormal termination, or abend, was so valuable to the programmer because it showed the contents of memory at the point-of-failure, then tracing every important function or routine, in-cluding the data, would add worlds of useful information to programs as they executed normally.

I was right. I soon found that tracing (auditing) every executing statement with its data was even better. With my "Harkins Trace," I could see exactly what was executing in the program, with its variables, and thus focus on the important main-line logic of any program that I traced, without looking at the source program.

Now, many programming languages have debuggers and tracers built right into the language and the operating system. RPG, for example, on the iSeries, has an extremely powerful trace/debug facility. You can set breakpoints and turn the debugging facility on or off at will. If you are working on a system with a language that has this kind of facility, you should not only be using it, you should become an expert in it. It will make you a much more effective and efficient programmer.

I have devised a software tool that automates the Harkins Trace. When I can't use it— say, on a consulting job where my tool is not available—I put in the trace manually. Here's how I do it: I make three sweeps through the program. In the first sweep, I audit (trace) file input/output. For instance, when I come across a READ statement in the program, I audit that statement. Then, every time that READ statement executes I know not only that it has in fact executed, but I can also see the data that was read.

I do the same with WRITE, UPDATE, and DELETE statements. That shows me where the input/output is.

Next I audit the conditional statements like IF. That makes it possible to see whether the statement has executed and see not only the contents of the data in the statement, but also whether the information is true or false.

Finally I take on the arithmetic and move statements, the guts of the program. For instance, for ADD, SUBTRACT, MULTIPLY, DIVIDE, MOVE, I can see that the instruction has executed, see the data used in the instruction, and learn whether the data was as I expected it to be.

As stunning as the visualization of the execution of any program and its data is, it is equally stunning for me to be able to work backward from when a program abends in order to see exactly the conditions that caused it to fail. (These conditions are almost always audited in the several pages of trace output before the abend occurs.)

After going through this procedure, I can just sit back and watch the trace output and then be able to tell exactly what went wrong with the program, and why, and best of all, how to correct it. Indeed, my audits do more. When I'm dealing with something like a warehouse distribution system and, say, a packer's creative packing techniques cause a glitch in the program, my trace output will identify the culprit. I can then tell my manager to provide more training for the errant packer (managers find this kind of sleuthing impressive).

I can often spend a week inserting my "Harkins Trace" audit statements into a key program. If you have the proper tools, that will be a week you don't have to spend. But if you don't, it is a week well spent. Providing yourself with a "hello" of every statement and piece of data that executed will let you master programs that it would take you much longer to master—or you'd be unable to master—without a trace.

The Ignored Hello

Whenever I used my trace, I was curious about how the programmers who followed me would react to the comments I'd put into the code. Sometimes, to their detriment, they just didn't get it. On one consulting job on Long Island, New York, I inserted the "Harkins Trace" into a 10,000-statement source program. The trace output helped me understand the actual program execution and then helped me add and implement some significant function for the client.

When I left this client, I turned the program over to another programmer—an excellent programmer and a good buddy of mine. He saw all my trace statements, and immediately deleted them, no doubt thinking they would get in his way. He then spent the next three days staring at the four-inch-thick compile listing of the program, trying to understand what the program did. I could have shown that to him easily in ten minutes, with the trace output, if only it hadn't been deleted.

Moral of the story: It is virtually impossible for anyone, no matter how intelligent, talented, and experienced, to know what a complex program will do. I am comfortable in that conclusion because the program (actually, its compiled, executable object program) will act very differently depending on the data or other inputs to the program. Anyone—anyone—who looks at a complex source program and thinks he knows how it will always execute will be proved wrong at some point— no doubt sooner than later.

$$ The Bottom Line $$

To master a complex program that is fat with thousands of lines of code, you must do three things. First, you must make sure you understand the particular business process (accounts payable, warehouse distribution, etc.) that the program deals with. Second, you must focus only on the key segment of the code that is of interest to you. Third, you must spend the time to put audits into the section of the program that you are working on—audits that enable you to see the program and data as it executes and learn the effect of your change, for good or ill.

Once you learn that you can easily understand virtually any source program by simply observing it as the object program executes with data, you are the master of most of the programs in your company's vast production program library. The rest is merely repetition and curiosity. Knowing how to audit a long, complex program will turn you into a very valuable, influential, and respected programmer and a desirable prospect for many other companies.

CHAPTER SEVENTEEN

"Good Enough" Programming for the Seasoned Programmer

Your personal standards for "good enough programming" should be significantly above the standards set by management and many of your programming peers, but you've got to recognize that there are times when tamping down your perfectionism is a necessity.

I've urged you to be the best programmer that you can be. Now that you have that down, welcome to the world of "good enough," in which your mission is to code to the business problem and no more. Think this might not be the strategy for you? In this chapter, I hope to bring you around.

"Good Enough" Is the Sign of a Professional

Forget about writing the perfect program. Your company can't afford to have you spend time doing that.

Virtually every job anywhere—and certainly corporate programming—requires a certain performance level. That is the level that management determines to be "good enough" performance. (Your personal standards for "good enough programming" should be significantly above the standards set by management and many of your programming peers, but you've got to recognize that there are times when tamping down your perfectionism is a necessity.)

Over time, your output as a programmer must exceed the amount the company expends for your work on the project. Remember, everything is economic. All of the programming projects that are assigned to you have some benefit that is probably estimated in monetary return or some productivity gain that can be translated to money.

The corporate programmer is often the biggest of the project's costs. If your projects consistently take much more time than expected, or more than those of other programmers doing similar work, you will eventually bear the consequences. Good-enough programming means cranking out lots of good-enough, if not gourmet, programs.

How to Measure "Good Enough"

There can be differences of opinion on what is a good-enough program, but the work clearly must be functional for its purpose, and not an embarrassment to its author. Good-enough programming starts, at the minimum, with following all of the company-set standards and procedures, as defined in a programming standards manual or common usage. There is no excuse for sloppy work, misspelled words, few or no comment statements, missing program objective, or abstruse and purposely confusing code.

Good-enough programming means, as I've pointed out in early chapters, not wasting time and energy concocting processing schemes or experiments to save a few milliseconds or nanoseconds in the running of a job. That kind of code tweaking was justified long ago, when processing cycles were expensive and precious, but it's not justified now.

This does not mean that good programmers are not aware of efficient and expected programming techniques, especially as applied to the relatively slow disk file processing. What it does mean is that the computer hardware is not the limiting factor anymore. Taking time and energy to scan through the millions of lines of source code already in your company's production libraries—code that runs your company's computerized business processes—will show you not only the requirements of good-enough coding, but probably superior coding.

When to Abandon Ship

No matter how many hours you've spent on your program, no matter what path you've taken or what logic you've used, forget it if it's a failure. Forget about "sunk cost"—the effort you've already put in. What you need to do is go on from there—to find the best path to your goal.

Let's say that you've written a program, put in a lot of time, but now you find that your logic was wrong or your information was wrong or incomplete. At any rate, the program doesn't work. New programmers tend to be so deeply invested in the work they've already done that they delay, for all too long, abandoning the program and starting afresh. Don't make that mistake. Good-enough programming practice tells you to have the wisdom to give up a bad program; don't go back and try to fix it.

When you test a program and it doesn't work, make one educated guess at a solution. If that doesn't work, don't keep guessing: That's the worst thing you can do. If your guess didn't work out, utilize a productivity tool that enables you to actually see what is happening inside the computer as your code and data execute. That guarantees that you will move forward in an organized, disciplined way. If you start guessing, guessing, guessing, you are simply adding to the time-cost you've already sunk into your program. Look carefully at where you are and where you've been, and cut off anything you've done that is of little value.

$$ Bottom Line $$

Superior programming is the "good enough" programming routinely produced by talented and experienced programmers—functional, understandable, and maintainable.

In my career, I have written probably thousands of good-enough programs, many as a highly paid programming consultant. Those programs met the expectations and objectives of the clients who asked for them and who paid for them. Believe me, as long as your programs work and are well documented, they're good enough.

CHAPTER EIGHTEEN

How Seasoned Programmers Stay at the Top of Their Game

There are no Olympic Games in programming, no best-of-the-best contests in which you can measure your performance against that of your peers. But, whether you sense it or not, you are always in a race with your colleagues. To motivate yourself to get and stay ahead of them, you must set your own benchmarks.

Competence is deceptive: It makes what's difficult (like turning a hopping ground ball into a double play) look smooth and effortless.

We're used to seeing champions in smooth, effortless action at athletic events. Their high achievement is immediately obvious because it is physical and can be measured against a set of expectations or world records that serve as benchmarks. Though it may not be immediately obvious, programmers can also use benchmarks to keep themselves at the top of their game.

Setting Your Own Benchmarks

Truly expert programmers make their work look easy, and they make sure the code they write is actually easy for the programmers who follow them to maintain or revise.

To attain this level—and, what's tougher, to sustain it—you must set your own benchmarks, because there are no local, regional, or national competitions coming up for which you can go into training.

I know, I know: Self-motivation, in the absence of overt competition, is hard to maintain. I've seen it in scores programming offices—employees who have stopped learning, stopped keeping an eye open for new developments that they could implement for the benefit of their company. They are getting by in their jobs, and they don't visualize themselves dropping behind other programmers in competence, because programmers are never set against each other in an obvious competition like a race. Most often, there is no clear and motivating signal to galvanize the corporate programmer into action.

There are no Olympic Games in programming, no best-of-the-best contests in which you can measure your performance against that of your peers. But, whether you sense it or not, you are always in a race with your colleagues. To motivate yourself to get and stay ahead of them, and to ward off a dead-end career, consider and use the following benchmarks:

- Of course, your first benchmark is your annual formal performance evaluation. If you do not receive—at the very least—an evaluation of "meets requirements," you are in big trouble. It surprises me how many programmers are content to get a "meets requirements" evaluation— which is either a C or a D, depending on the number of your company's ranking categories. Performance evaluations are directly tied to pay raises, and only the highly rated programmers are normally considered for promotion or for other corporate positions.

- Another performance benchmark is being promoted to another programmer title, which normally means a bump in your compensation. In your early years as a programmer, you should expect to be promoted to the next job title within about two years, or wonder—and ask your manager—why you are not being promoted.

- Yet another performance benchmark is whether your manager asks you to work on difficult and critical projects. Allied with that indication of competence is this benchmark: You should be able to work on difficult projects without asking or receiving constant help from your peers.

When Your Benchmark Is Another Programmer

At the moment, you may have no perceived competitors threatening your status in the IT department. But at any moment, your manager may hire a Tom Terrific who will force an agonizing reappraisal of you and the other programmers at your company.

I've seen the Tom Terrific factor in action. Years ago, I was asked by my systems engineering manager at IBM to find out why a particular installation (in which an IBM System/34 was replacing a Honeywell System H200 computer) was way behind schedule.

I didn't have time to work on the project myself, but I agreed to have a weekly luncheon meeting with the CFO and the IT manager at the installation. They had already spent several months on it, they said, but the conversion would require six person-years to complete.

I suggested to the CFO that the programmers probably had lots of slush (extra) time built into their application estimates for the conversion. I vowed to get a detailed (and real) estimate of the conversion effort required the next week.

At our second weekly meeting, I brought in a homemade benchmark—my Master Program List program. (I had developed this project management productivity tool many years before to document the programs of each company that was installing an IBM computer.) This gave us a gauge by which we could track every programmer's performance and the overall progress of the project, and therefore the project's possible end date.

I loaded my trusty program on the System/34, and the next week the programmers keyed each application and each and every program to which they were assigned into the system for management review.

To my surprise and disappointment, the results showed that there were indeed six years of programming person-work left on the project, and that each of the six programmers had about one person-year of conversion work left.

I received similar doleful news at the fourth weekly meeting: The updated Master Program List still showed six years of programming person-work left on the project. Indeed, so little progress had been made that one of the programmers had left in disgust and frustration. His replacement programmer, named Tom, was starting that afternoon.

Little change at the fifth meeting: The Master Program List still showed almost six person-years of work left. The good news was that the new programmer, Tom, had miraculously done six weeks of his assigned Master Program List programs on his very first week on the job.

The CFO and I were flabbergasted. We went to meet this virtuoso programmer, only to find a roly-poly guy in baggy pants who was at least fifteen years older than the rest of us. We had to interrupt him, because he was working so intently.

At my sixth and last weekly luncheon meeting, the IT manager showed the CFO and me of the results of the latest update of the Master Program List. Somehow, there were only five and a half years of programming person-work left. Incredibly, virtually all of the programmers were racing through their conversion programs, perhaps trying to keep up with Tom Terrific. Tom had been able to demonstrate not only much-needed programming skill and focus, but leadership in helping the other programmers bypass their problems and succeed. Tom set and raised the standard by working up to his personal programming standard.

The CFO reported this fantastic turn of events back to my SE manager, and I got an IBM night-on-the-town award for dinner with my wife at the best French restaurant in Philadelphia. And I got it because of the pace set by the front-runner, Tom Terrific.

$$ The Bottom Line $$

Even if your job is easy, you've got to keep pushing—to work faster, to learn new techniques. That's hard to do: It's human nature to relax into a comfortable pace. To stay motivated, you may want to set particular benchmarks by which you measure your performance. To keep yourself striving, it may help to understand that you are, in fact, in competition with your colleagues inside and outside the company, not only to win promotions but just to stay on the job. Right now, downsizing may lurk in the heart of your CFO. If that's the case, attention will be paid to your speed and sophistication relative to that of your programming peers. Whether you sense it or not, you are always in a long-distance race.

CHAPTER NINETEEN

Self-Management Tips
for the Seasoned Professional

My understanding of programmers' temperament and my experience on the job have led me to the conclusion that the optimal number of programmers on a project team is one—unless you have a programming genius as a partner.

You are ultimately responsible for your own projects. Of course, that doesn't mean that you're responsible just for coding. It means that you're responsible for time management, co-worker relations, and your own workload as well.

Help at Your Own Convenience

Since your programming performance is constantly being measured, you must strictly ration the amount of time you spend helping other programmers. There is a difference between helping a fellow programmer and carrying him. I gladly help other programmers, as others have helped me. That means that when I can spare the time from a project, I help anyone who asks for my help. But the time I spend helping them is at my convenience, not theirs.

When I am focused on a project, I do not allow fellow programmers to come into my office and sit down and interrupt me. If that happens, I simply get up and politely tell my colleague that I'm on my way to the bathroom. (This may seem awkward and abrupt, but it is a classic time-management technique.) If you are relegated to working in a cube, and the cube has room for a guest chair, take the guest chair out.

If you are unfortunate enough to have to share a cube with another programmer, and the programmer turns out to be a "talker," you must ask to have your situation changed. Remember that when it is time for your annual performance evaluation, you cannot excuse poor performance with the complaint, "He made me listen."

Recognize a Great Programming Team When You See It

My understanding of programmers' temperament and my experience on the job have led me to the conclusion that the optimal number of programmers on a project team is one—unless you have a programming genius as a partner. In that case, the optimal size of the programming team is most definitely two.

It can happen—finding a genius for a partner. For many years I teamed up with Garry Reinhard to write the code that became IBM's first online apparel programming package. Our strengths combined magically. I supplied the idea and design of the package, and was skilled at working smoothly with IBM management, and Garry provided unbelievably powerful coding and systems integration.

Another important reason that we succeeded as a team is that we were both driven to work seven days a week to make the project successful. If you are a driven programmer who will work overtime to accomplish your goals but are paired with a colleague who is a nine-to- fiver, your collaboration will be unpleasant, and probably unsuccessful.

Finding someone in corporate programming who can complement your skills is a goal that you should be striving for throughout your career. Many of the tiny startup companies that became multi-billion-dollar software or technology companies started with exactly two partners, each of whom complemented the skills of the other.

Dare to Say No

You can say no when your manager proposes that you collaborate with someone you consider incompetent. Just say no—politely. That's what I did when, as a consultant at an apparel company, my manager asked me to work with the worst programmer in the office. (I had asked to be paired with a different, and talented, colleague.) I told my boss (respectfully) that I would rather work alone, even though the project would take longer that way. Eventually, my chosen partner was allowed to work with me part-time. Even if that hadn't happened, I knew it was better to work alone than to work with someone I couldn't depend on.

Your manager and his superiors are focused on successfully completing critical projects, not on just keeping every programmer occupied. Make sure you keep the bottom line in the forefront of every conversation with your boss. It will make him or her see the reason for your "no" much more clearly.

$$ The Bottom Line $$

Look out for your own interests. You may shrink from appearing rude when your colleagues drop into your working space for a few minutes of R and R. But you've got to get across the message that you don't want to be interrupted. If your manager proposes to team you with another programmer for development work, and you believe that programmer isn't competent enough, tell your manager, politely, " I don't believe we have the right resources for this project." Then ask to work with a colleague who matches you in zeal and whose skills complement your own. Your manager will listen.

CHAPTER TWENTY

Spotting Opportunities, Skirting Land Mines

Management styles are as varied as the personalities of the managers themselves. However, when a manager starts a topic with "I think you should consider..." he is invariably alerting you to focus on an important issue, and you had better address it.

Opportunities abound in our industry, but you have to recognize them when they come along. And, to avoid explosions, you must also learn to spot the land mines that lurk beneath a "suggestion" or a request for opinion from your boss.

What Is Your Manager Really Saying?

"I think you should consider..." This is the polite form of "I want you to..."

Management styles are as varied as the personalities of the managers themselves. However, when a manager starts a topic with "I think you should consider..." he is invariably alerting you to focus on an important issue, and you had better address it.

Common sense? Apparently not. I've worked with bright and talented colleagues who were mystifyingly deaf to suggestion and blind to opportunity, even after many years in the business.

Here's an example of a missed opportunity. On one consulting job I was assigned to an empty desk in the accounting department, where I could observe everyone and listen to all the office chatter, even through my requisite earplugs. One day, the CFO said to one of the trainee accountants: "I think you should consider taking some accounting courses at the community college at night, and of course the company will pay for them." The employee responded that he would try to find time, but that he was really busy after work.

Obviously, the manager was giving his employee a significant clue that he needed additional education. He was even offering to pay for it. Perhaps he was giving this clue to prepare the employee for a promotion. Perhaps he was alerting the employee that his current job performance was inadequate. Either way, the employee should have discerned that even a soft suggestion from a boss has weight behind it. His reaction should have been graceful acquiescence, or some acceptable alternate arrangement. He offered neither.

Your programming manager may see a coming departmental need for skills that you don't have, and "suggest" that you acquire them. He or she may need to send you to work in a location away from your hometown, or to work on a less-than-exciting project. The programmers who respond positively to their manager's request will be the ones who get the promotions, the raises, and the consideration for corporate jobs. So don't take what may seem like a light suggestion lightly—not from a boss.

Tiptoeing Through a Minefield

I had been consulting for months at a company that was implementing a very advanced computer system when one day the CEO and the CFO invited the IT manager and me to lunch for an update. After lunch and a positive update, the CEO sprang an unexpected question on us (the CFO had already been briefed). He told us that the company was going into a new mail-order business, with advertising in national magazines, and he wanted to know how many consumer responses he thought we would get from the magazine ad campaign, to get an idea of the computer processing we might need to be prepared for. The CEO asked us all to write our guesses on a paper napkin, so we could discuss the work to be planned. When the napkins were turned over, the CFO's guess was 30,000 responses, mine was 20,000 responses, and the IT manager's was . . . incredibly. . . zero. The big bosses' displeasure and chagrin were palpable.

The IT manager should have made allowance for our bosses' egos. He was being honest: He didn't think the ads would pull responses. When it comes to discussing your own work with your boss, straight talk is the byword. But when you are putting your boss on the line and in the spotlight, brutal honesty is not the best policy. Obviously these top officials were enthusiastic about their idea. To declare that the ads would generate no responses at all was a slap in the face to both of them. Prudence and an understanding of human nature should have kept my colleague from insulting his bosses with an answer that showed contempt for their idea.

Shortly afterward, my colleague was fired.

Opportunities to Spread Your Wings

Perhaps once or twice in the span of your working career you may be presented with a golden opportunity for fame and fortune—if you recognize it. It's possible to be blind to opportunity, as my fellow systems engineers were back in the seventies—even though our company was encouraging us to seize this chance. It turned out to be the biggest opportunity of my career—and I seized it because IBM asked me to.

The Scenario

In the early 1970s, most companies had just installed, or were in the process of installing, their first (mainframe) computer. There were tens of thousands of companies computerizing their businesses for the first time, and many of them were small companies. Each company wrote most, if not all, of the programs that ran its business in-house, because there were virtually no application-related software packages available.

This was good news and bad news for IBM. The good news was that virtually all the customers were clamoring for IBM education (at a fee) and an IBM systems engineer (at an astronomical fee) to help their new programmers write and install their new computers. I remember working for many months splitting my billable systems engineering tasks among several customers' shops and driving for an hour from one to the other, with no time to eat lunch. My boss forgot to think about my lunch when he scheduled my time with the key customers.

The bad news for IBM was that there were not enough newly trained customer programmers or IBM systems engineers to install those thousands of first mainframe computers effectively, no matter how hard we worked. This led to some really severe installation problems and threatened to slow the pace of IBM computer customer acceptance and payment for the computers. Most of the IBM systems were rented then, not purchased, so IBM couldn't start the rent until the customer accepted the computer.

The Solution

Some genius at IBM headquarters (and I am not being sarcastic) thought of a fantastic, creative way to solve all of these problems quickly, at almost no cost. He or she came up with the idea of finding the very best customer in every industry that already had an excellent set of computer software applications running on the company IBM computer. IBM had found that in virtually every industry there was at least one already installed and supremely happy customer with excellent software applications.

Could that best customer be a showcase installation for the hundreds or thousands of companies essentially just like it in the industry? And could that customer provide its proven software (for a nice fee) to all the other companies in the industry who wanted it? Yes, this was feasible.

Could IBM persuade the showcase customer to accept a nice royalty on the software that the other companies would pay IBM? And would the showcase customer like IBM to generate some impressive publicity about how successful and advanced the customer was in using this leading technology? Probably, yes. Most of the corporate CEOs were definitely Mr. Outside personalities, and were pleased at the chance to showcase their company's strengths.

Now all IBM had to do was to get someone who was really good at programming—perhaps the programmer who had written that superb application for that "best customer"—engaged in this effort. The accomplished programmer would spend lots of time and effort to review the system and bring it up to IBM standards for program distribution. He or she would also write clear IBM manuals needed to install and support this model system, exhaustively test it, and package it for IBM distribution worldwide. And support it after that, of course. Oh, and do all this work in the evening, without extra pay.

Could IBM possibly persuade a gullible IBM systems engineer to bite at this one? Well, yes—at least me.

The Message

Soon after the IBM genius came up with this plan, every SE in the country found, in his or her mailbox (this was before e-mail) a brightly colored flyer from IBM headquarters extolling the potential virtues and benefits of the Installed User Program (IUP)—benefits for IBM, the customers, and, potentially, for the systems engineer who was interested in applying himself or herself to such an effort (a big after-work project). All the flyers but mine promptly flew into wastebaskets.

I talked to my manager about possibly doing an IUP with a small apparel company that had just installed its first computer and where I had done most of the programming. My manager gave me quiet encouragement to do it on my off hours, so my billing performance would not drop below forty hours a week. I chose to do it.

Yes, there was no immediate payoff, and doing this work, without payment, after a grueling overtime week at IBM, seemed ludicrous to all the other systems engineers. But I took the position that this idea, a groundbreaking idea at the time, would lead to some sort of reward, eventually.

And it did. After I'd created the Apparel Business System, the first interactive software package created for the apparel industry, I got to fly around the world presenting my first real software product of IBM quality. I've seen it in use in hundreds of companies (indeed, its offspring products are still being sold). I even got a $10,000 award as a royalty for doing it (which I figure works out to about $5 an hour). I also got at least some respect from IBM: The company presented me with an IBM national award on a stage in San Francisco (my fifteen seconds of fame) and created a National Apparel Support Center—a beautiful office overlooking a lake—where I and my partner, Garry Reinhard, could support the package worldwide. All because I simply said yes, I would consider the genius's proposal. The rest of the systems engineers, who tossed the opportunity away, got to go home.

$$ The Bottom Line $$

An opportunity that could enhance—even change—your career may not show up accompanied by the sound of trumpets. The potential rewards of a project you are offered or that you hear about may not be quantifiable, or even foreseeable. But any opportunity or challenge that requires intensive effort and that stretches your ability is likely to pay off in ways you can't anticipate. Don't shrink from a challenge.

Section 3

Mastering the Corporate Culture

It Takes More Than Business Savvy and Coding Skill to Get to the Top

CHAPTER TWENTY ONE

Slipping Into a New Corporate Culture

*Programmers expect to make transitions every few years through-
out their career. How do you adapt to these situations in a polite,
professional, and productive manner? This chapter discusses four
rules of engagement that you need to know.*

Back when I went into information technology, we programmers
rarely had to exercise our adaptability genes. We actually wanted
to keep a good job as long as we could.

It took twenty-one years before I left IBM, the company I joined
right out of college—the job I assumed would be a lifetime post. And the
transition was jarring. I went from a corporation with 300,000 employees, legendary decorum, vast financial resources, and world-class procedures to a software startup housed in a corner of a factory in a crime-
ridden section of Philadelphia. It had a payroll of six, barely enough
income to pay our salaries, an unruly staff, and—since there were no
company standards or procedures—wonderful creative freedom.

These days, programmers expect to make transitions like that every few years throughout their career. How do you adapt to these situations in a polite, professional, and productive manner? You follow the
"A's" of good behavior.

Don't Be the Arrogant Newbie

When you start your new job, pay attention to the vibes you're giving off. Whenever a newcomer signs on, the established programmers
in the department inevitably take stock, get ready for comparisons.
Nobody welcomes a hotshot who might show him up as lazy or

unproductive. And if the hotshot is not only talented but sharp-edged, collegiality between the newcomer and the veterans never takes hold.

So watch out that you don't convey condescension in any of your dealings with your new co-workers. Don't try to "loosen up" a decorous office with the freewheeling bluntness you prized in your old shop. And hold off on testing the company ways until you've gained some experience in your new environment and know that you're considered a valuable employee. It's important that you adopt your new company's IT culture and standards before attempting to dazzle your manager and your colleagues with your skills and try to change the way they operate.

Don't Assume That You Know What Got You the Job

One of my clients, a large apparel company, was looking for an experienced programmer who could support a very complex and critical warehousing and distribution function. As a programmer who had already worked on that hectic and business-critical function, which shipped millions of dollars of product every day, my perspective was that the company simply needed someone really good.

But one day, walking past the office of the IT manager, I heard her discussing the job with a staffer from the Human Resources department. "What's the key hiring requirement?" the HR person asked. The answer stunned me: "We want a programmer with an even disposition."

Obviously, the manager considered skill a given. She had gone to the next level—finding a person whose behavior had shown that he or she could deal with the stress of the job, and do so without stirring up the environment.

If you were the person hired for the job, you might never know the final deciding factor that brought you through the front door. Don't act as if you do.

Avoid Ramming Your Ideas Down Everyone's Throat

You may bring to your new company ideas that would prove quite valuable—especially to a small or rapidly growing shop. A small or fast-growing company, with its shortage of experience and talent, may have no consistently applied standards and procedures; management allows the programmers' and managers' individual experience to prevail. Even the members of a programming team may use different standards. To you, an IT department like this may seem to be operating in semi-chaos.

In these situations, you can nudge the performance of your colleagues upward by using the standards and procedures you were trained to employ in your old job. If you're lucky, someone in authority will notice.

When I was a consulting programmer for a large software company, we used a set of detailed, handwritten program turnover documents when we went out to our clients' offices. (Not all of those client companies had a software change management system. That's why we couldn't simply employ a standard change management software package.)

At my new company, there were no consistent or particularly effective manual change management procedures. That led to mistakes in the programming projects turned over to production. So, on my new job, I started using manual program turnover documents similar to my previous company's (uncopyrighted) documents.

To my surprise, the systems analyst that I worked with adopted them and asked all the programmers on the team to use them. The project turnover procedure went much more smoothly than it had before, and now the disaster recovery and rollback procedures were written down, so they'd be available immediately if some problem occurred. I still find it satisfying, when I consult at that company years later, to see quite a few of the programmer productivity procedures I brought to the company still in use in this rapidly growing company. I didn't invent them; I just passed them on—simply by using them—from my prior work experience to others who were not aware of those effective procedures.

If you come to a company with really effective tools and techniques, be bold enough to try them on your first project and see how your manager reacts. If he likes them, he may propagate them throughout the department. If not, then you can adapt to the company's procedures, even if they're not as efficient as the ones you're used to.

Accept the Status Quo...for Now

New programmers who are hired to work in a shop using an older version of the language are obviously obligated to learn that older version. Don't grumble about it—that insults your older colleagues. Learn what you must with good grace.

New programmers can almost certainly be taught the older language of the shop with a small amount of in-house training. The many working production programs in the company library and the company databases are the models for this education, together with a comprehensive programming standard manual.

If you find yourself being taught a language that you think is antiquated, keep you mouth shut and cheerfully apply yourself to the task. You're part of a team. You accepted the job. There's time enough for rocking the boat later, after you've proved yourself and built your relationships.

And here's a note to "old guard" programmers who are uncomfortable with the invasion of younger programmers touting the new languages: Remember that learning new languages is a good way to avoid being classified as a dodo and the best way to gain a résumé that will command respect in the job market when you need to find another job. It may take only a matter of days of education for you, the experienced programmer, to get up to a reasonable level of competence in the new programming language—a level that will give you the capacity to maintain a key program in the new language in an emergency.

So when new programmers come into your shop, don't be too lethargic or "too busy" to take whatever classes in the new languages your manager offers. This is your opportunity to learn a new language one program at a time, modeling your techniques after the production program in the new language. And don't be too stiff-necked to ask for help from a newcomer whose language expertise is more current than yours.

$$ The Bottom Line $$

Slip into your new company's culture gracefully. Pay attention to the boundaries your manager and his manager have set up, refrain from coming on like a hotshot, and cheerfully set out to learn whatever new (or old) languages your manager needs you to learn. You'll build lasting relationships with your co-workers when you do.

CHAPTER TWENTY TWO

Mentors and Mentees

The mentor and the mentee complement each other: The mentor has the power, the access, and the ideas, and the mentee has the technical ability to turn the mentor's ideas into reality.

Having a mentor in your chosen profession is almost as good as being born rich.

If you don't happen to be wellborn, having a mentor is the next best thing. He (or she) will give you the precious gift of encouragement; will clue you in on how to get ahead politically at your company; and will bring your name up at meetings as someone who's ready to tackle a major project. He or she has the power to make things happen. And so it behooves every programmer to search for and cultivate mentors who have power and connections, and who will favor him or her with a hand up. Mentors make the difference for a mid-career professional. Often, your one big break is the direct result of their actions.

Why Do They Bother?

You may wonder why a powerful executive would want to take the time to mentor. The good news is that, over my long career, I have found that many executives are actually looking for talent to help them carry out their mission. The mentor and the mentee complement each other: The mentor has the power, the access, and the ideas, and the mentee has the technical ability to turn the mentor's ideas into reality.

Consider my relationship with one of my mentors at IBM, Robert D. White.

Bob White was an IBM consultant to the apparel and footwear industry during my time at IBM, and one of the seven corporate industry consultants reporting to IBM headquarters. Bob had responsibility for the strategic direction of IBM's development and support of computing in many thousands of apparel companies, but he had only three regional directors reporting to him. He had to depend on the "field" of branch office IBMers to actually implement software products.

I got to work directly with Bob when I developed my first IBM software Installed User Program (IUP) product. The product was about ready to be announced, but first it had to go to Corporate for pricing, a product name, and legal review. I had done all the technical work on the package, but I couldn't seem to find a good name for it, so when HQ came up with the name "Apparel Business System" and a good competitive price, I was immediately impressed with IBM corporate management and with Bob White, who had picked that name.

While many IBM systems engineers thought that the IBMers who couldn't program were "overhead" and out of the mainstream, I learned how vital these non-programmers were to the company's success. I got to attend many of the seminars Bob would give to CEOs about the state of the worldwide apparel industry and IBM's strategic direction. That was spellbinding stuff for me; Bob could hold the interest of a roomful of CEOs.

Bob eventually became an invaluable mentor to me, encouraging me to develop IBM software products that he personally presented to corporate IBM. He had found someone in the field to implement his vision, and I had found someone in IBM headquarters to help me expand my own vision. And our skills were so different that we complemented each other, rather than interfering with or second-guessing each other.

Yet, as I've said, most of my programming colleagues did not recognize Bob for the potential mentor that he was. They did not grasp the fact that he was in a position to exert major, positive impact on any programmer's career. Maybe they didn't see him as mentor material because he was so far away in the New York corporate office. I don't know, but they missed out on a wonderful opportunity.

You Learn More Than Your Business

Bob taught me many things about corporate life that were helpful to a lowly corporate programmer like me. I studied his dress, his suits, and his manner with his colleagues and his subordinates. I paid respectful attention to his ability to get me to respond gladly to what he wanted me to do. I learned that to go to a national conference in Atlanta, where we presented my IBM software product, I didn't need to take ten days' worth of clothing (mostly suits). It was news to me that a briefcase and a carry-on bag would suffice, because you could get your suits cleaned and shirts laundered by the hotel and IBM would pay for it. Also, I was using my weekends to fly to conferences; Bob's advice was to fly on company time, and to take a minimum of clothing, because the company really wanted its employees to be comfortable when traveling, and productive. Didn't I know that? Hadn't my boss told me that?

No. It took my mentor to tell me that.

You Learn More of Your Business

Bob White also taught me to think about the big picture and to consider his vision of the current and future trends affecting IBM and its apparel customers, rather than just focusing on my branch office job as an IBM systems engineer. Bob had started out, like most top executives at IBM, as a lowly branch office marketing representative (salesman); his ability to surpass his sales quota and his ability to sell himself to upper management got him quickly promoted to higher levels in the branch and the company. Bob ultimately traveled much of the world, sometimes with me in tow, and he wowed them everywhere.

How to Find a Mentor

The corporate programmer can most easily meet and mingle with potential powerful mentors within the company by working on and presenting high-visibility projects for top management.

The programmer can meet and cultivate potential mentors by going to seminars, conferences, trade shows, and meetings outside his company, as well as through his network and by judiciously floating his résumé or availability to the best headhunters.

There are literally hundreds of potential mentors in large companies, and as an IT programmer, you can interface with many of them every day as they request support and new projects from IT. When you deliver for a manager, at any level, you will be considered and perhaps sought by him or her later.

If you are lucky, your manager will be your mentor. I know a programmer who worked for a boss who was so encouraging about her talent that he brought in a classified ad for a junior systems analyst at another company and urged her to try for the job. Now *that* was a mentor.

My Best Mentor

At IBM I had scores of good managers, many of whom turned out to be mentors. Of a good lot, the most superb was Hank Guckes.

Hank, an IBM systems engineer, had a rare combination of virtues—excellent programming skills and wonderful "people skills." He was chosen to manage the Apparel Business System/370, the very complex IBM software development project that Garry Reinhard and I worked on seven days a week for almost a year.

Hank helped us greatly by communicating effectively with IBM corporate management (keeping the brass off our backs by reassuring them that all was going well) and by leaving us alone to do the tough design and programming work. We worked harder for him because we knew he understood us.

You as a Mentor

Just as you've had mentors who have significantly helped you, you have an obligation to be a mentor to others.

I like to believe that I was a mentor, at least briefly, to Garry Reinhard. I helped Garry get into IBM because I needed him to help me create the IBM Apparel Business System software product, then I watched him accelerate through many opportunities—so much so that he has become a mentor of sorts to me.

Be prepared to give a significant amount of your time and energy to mentor others, as others have given time and energy to mentor you. However, you will have to guard against those who will utilize your time and talents without applying themselves enough to deserve your mentoring. To achieve a successful and lasting relationship, the mentor and the mentee must both give of themselves. And the mentee must be worthy of his or her mentor's time and trust.

$$ The Bottom Line $$

A talented and hardworking programmer who connects with an influential mentor has the greatest chance for success. Indeed, keen as I am on the virtues of talent and hard work (and some people think I'm so high on them that I'm over the top), if I had to choose between being talented and hardworking, but not having a mentor, or being average in skill and zeal but having a powerful mentor, I would choose the latter.

You have many opportunities to find valuable and powerful mentors who will project your career upward as you, in turn, help them with their careers. Placing yourself in high-visibility and high-potential situations, specifically projects that are very important to upper management, will put you in the spotlight for probable selection by a well-connected mentor as he or she moves up inside or outside your company.

CHAPTER TWENTY THREE

How Do You Deal with the End User?

"Having rapport with users, building their trust, means that the end users don't feel as if IT is shoving something down their throats," Dan Goldstein says. "That matters, because if the users don't buy into something you're introducing, it is not going to work. They can make or break any system."

Dealing with an end user can be tricky. Even as an experienced programmer you will have end user encounters that will require all of your expertise and finesse to facilitate. To help you visualize some of the situations you might encounter, this chapter presents some tips from two IT veterans—Jean Kopan and Dan Goldstein, both of whom have gained perspective on the problem not only as programmers but also as high-level IT managers.

"Yes" Is Not Always the Correct Answer

Jean Kopan, vice-president of technical development at a software development and consulting company in suburban Philadelphia, has the following advice:

"When a user comes to you with a request, you should not just transcribe that request into programming. The request may be counterproductive.

"For instance, let's say someone in the order entry department says, 'I don't really see why I have to key in this order classification code. I don't want to key it in anymore. Take it off the screen.'

"But everyone in the sales department is using that classification code to decide how well certain classes of orders are selling. So if you take out that code, there'll be a ripple effect. You cannot always just do what the user wants. To respond intelligently to his request, you need to understand the business of the company, what the other users are doing, and how this request may affect other parts of the company."

You may notice that Jean has just affirmed my oft-stated axiom that you cannot be a good programmer without having a thorough knowledge of the flow of your company or client's business. In the situation she described, you wouldn't be savvy enough to say "no" unless you understood the business.

Courtesy Is a Mandate

Another piece of advice from Jean is about how programmers should relate to end users.

"Sometimes," Jean explains, "programmers don't seem to understand that users are their customers. I've gone to some shops where the IT department treats users as if they're nuisances. The attitude is, 'You're a hindrance; you're asking me for something; you're bothering me.' This is a really bad attitude to have. Some programmers think it's okay to put their priorities ahead of all the users that are on the system, even if they drag the system down. I've told programmers, 'This is not the way it's supposed to be. You are serving them. They are running the company. You are helping them to run the company.'"

Personally, I can't stress this point enough to new (and experienced) programmers. The business exists to make money; you exist to help the business make money. If you thwart the ability of the business to make money, you deserve to be fired.

Relationship Building is a Process, Not an Isolated Task

Dan Goldstein—who rose, without any formal education in programming, from a $58-a-week job (in 1964) wiring control panels for

IBM accounting machines to a high rank in IT management—also stresses "communication and respect" when dealing with an end user. Dan, now retired, spent his last twenty-seven IT years with a large manufacturing company as the data processing manager.

He notes: "In that job I got to install and support several computers in widespread locations in the States and in the Caribbean. I got to hire and work with programmers and to work directly with the company owners. I tried to hire programmers with skill, but also with a personality that let them relate to and communicate well with end users and with management.

"In the early days, I was a one-man shop—programmer, DP manager, systems person, and sometimes operator when the operator was out," Dan says. "But that meant that I got to understand the entire application. For instance, when I had to put in a cutting-room incentive payroll, I had to know what a cutting room was (where stacks of clothing fabric were manually cut into clothing parts) and know what the cutters did.

"Today, programming seems to me to be segmented, and the programmer only knows a tiny piece of applications. Companies seem to want programmers to sit in an office rather than go out into the company. I made it clear that IT was a service department. I knew the name of every person in the company that I worked with, including the factory employees. But in my last job, the new middle managers who came in made it clear to me that they thought I was spending too much time working with the end users—I should be sitting in an office instead, writing code to implement processes that I hadn't observed. That's the idea today, and it's ridiculously counterproductive; that's why programmers today can't see the forest for the trees.

"Having rapport with users, building their trust, means that the end users don't feel as if IT is shoving something down their throats," Dan says. "That matters, because if the users don't buy into something you're introducing, it is not going to work. They can make or break any system.

"The power of the computer today is immense, and the younger programmers use lots of fancy op codes, but they really don't know what is going on inside the CPU. You could say, 'Set up a system,' and they wouldn't know where to begin in setting up the databases, master files, and integrated systems for a major application. That is primarily because they are not involved with the end users. They don't know the *jobs of the end users, so they can't see how all those jobs integrate to get the job done in the company."*

You have to understand your business and be willing to work respectfully with your end users. In my opinion, anything less creates mistrust, and that is a disaster in the making.

$$ The Bottom Line $$

When you got your first programming job, it was all you could do to learn the ropes. Now that you are more experienced, your boss should (and, if you're lucky, *will)* expect you to interact with end users. Use the tips in this chapter to make your interactions with end users professional and productive.

CHAPTER TWENTY FOUR

When You Get a Really Bad Boss

If you find yourself in a mid-career position dealing with a really bad boss, try not to despair. There is hope and there are choices— choices you might not have had when you were just getting out of college.

You may have the extreme bad luck to be stuck with a bad boss on your first job, or early in your career. I was fortunate: I didn't get a miserable manager until I'd been in the field long enough to build up an unshakeable belief in my own programming competence. If you find yourself in a mid-career position dealing with a really bad boss, try not to despair. There is hope and there are choices, choices you might not have had when you were just getting out of college. To get a handle on how you can cope, read on.

Bad Bosses Happen

The worst bosses often rule by public humiliation. They rant. They feel the need to bulldoze their subordinates—to make their authority manifest. Such a boss may not be quenchable, for he is dealing from a position of strength. Only a company owner or someone working with the acquiescence of management can get away with operating like that. (Out-of-control manager behavior is less and less visible in big companies, whose human resources department monitors how employees are treated in many ways.)

The bad manager I finally drew after fifteen years at IBM wasn't a ranter (ranting would never have been tolerated at IBM). But his quiet oppression was more dangerous, because I wanted to keep this job, and he had the power to force me into leaving it.

When I first started working for this manager, it seemed that he was ready, willing, and eager to stick it to me. I don't know why, but it didn't matter; he was all over me for his own reasons. He didn't seem to care about my excellent work record, or my IBM awards, or the software products that I had developed, or the countries I had visited for IBM, or my top-employee evaluation rating, or even that I knew the branch manager, who was his boss. He was interested in my doing things exactly his way, and how and where he wanted it done, with exactly the results he expected. He was clearly interested in achieving his goals, but he didn't ask about or consider my goals.

I checked with my systems-engineer buddies, and they weren't thrilled either, so I thought perhaps he simply was not aware of how we operated, or—even more important—how IBM operated: The first principle of the IBM Code of Conduct was "Respect for the Individual" in the manager/employee relationship.

No, he apparently just wanted to do things his way, and he had the power to do it, and he was going to show us—and apparently especially me—that he was indeed the boss (which we never disputed). Perhaps his problem with me was that I was spending time overseas and not on the branch customer accounts...or something. And no amount of attempted cooperation or conciliation or rational thinking could change things.

So it was war.

Sometimes, the System Will Save You

My first, and obvious, tactic was to avoid a frontal assault. I needed to find some clever feint, like the tactics used by all those famous generals in wars past to surprise and then decisively defeat the enemym But I was only a private, and the strategy for victory eluded me. So I bided my time and hoped for help. I had evaluated my war assets and liabilities, as well as my opponent's, and I determined that my manager had more firepower than I did and that I had best wait for help while trying to survive as best I could.

Then one day the branch office mailbox of every employee held a notice of the annual IBM employee evaluations. Each year, IBM formally evaluated every employee, and the employee evaluated his manager, his manager's manager, and the IBM corporate office.

For the first time I sensed a whiff of unease in my manager when he saw me. My SE buddies seemed to pick that up also as we discussed the general conditions in the office this year compared with those in the office at this time in previous years.

We all were formally evaluated. We filled out our evaluations of management, and off they went, as always, to IBM Corporate in Armonk, New York, for analysis.

Somewhere in the sea of employees' positive evaluations of management there must have been at least one red flag that popped out in Armonk. For soon afterward, an emissary from the corporate office unexpectedly showed up at our branch, asking the way to the branch manager's and my manager's offices. Several weeks after that, our bad manager had silently stolen away.

We programmers had won the war with only one remote ally, partly because of our good reputations and proven contributions to IBM, but mostly because of IBM itself. The company had implemented checks and balances for just that sort of situation; when given the needed information, IBM took the needed corrective action.

My advice to you? Look for avenues within your company to air your grievances. You never know what might happen.

Sometimes, You Have to Save Yourself

When you get a boss that you simply cannot work with, especially if you are sure it is not your fault, then you must move on. If you have proved your value and productivity in your company, you can probably ask your boss for a graceful (for you both) transfer elsewhere in the department or in the company.

If you are working in a large company, programmers and programming managers turn over constantly, and that gives you the opportunity to ask for a transfer to the IT manager or application of your choice. In the new department you will learn another business function, perhaps learn new programming techniques, work with new programmers and perhaps a better manager, and become reinvigorated—and more valuable—in the process. That is one reason not to become the indispensable programmer in one area of the business.

If waiting and watching for a new opportunity doesn't work, you have little to lose by going over your boss's head and requesting a meeting with your manager's manager. When a boss is hostile (or even malicious) toward you, it is his manager's job to listen to you and take considered action to keep you in the company, if possible.

The IT manager in a large IT department will probably be the VP of IT or the CIO. In a smaller company, it may be the owner or the president. In either case, that manager will most likely have hired your manager, and he probably didn't expect personnel problems when he made that decision. At the least, this executive-level manager should be able to have your manager tone down his hostility toward you until some accommodation or exit strategy can be made for you. Executive management needs to be focused on the objectives of upper management, and you and your manager are expected to contribute to accomplishing your superiors' goals, not to be hindering the process.

It should give you confidence to know that you are valuable, for your acquired knowledge is irreplaceable, at least for some time. When a key programmer leaves a company after years developing and supporting critical projects, there is simply no way to immediately replace the knowledge loss. In fact, that brain drain could be worth tens of thousands of dollars.

$$ The Bottom Line $$

When you draw a bad boss, much of your power to improve your situation is vested in the weight of your reputation and the fact that your boss cannot afford to look bad to his manager. That knowledge is a powerful ally for you, especially if you use it with finesse. Before you choose to leave the company, go to your boss's boss and speak up; management may resolve your quandary for you. And if you do move on, do it gracefully, while informing senior management and the human resources department of your unresolved conflict. That is information that they don't like to hear, but they understand their need to know.

CHAPTER TWENTY FIVE

A Raise and a Promotion In-House

Coming into your manager's office with a solid offer from another company and using it to negotiate a raise and/or promotion is good strategy. But any experienced programmer knows that meeting your manager armed with nothing but the threat that you'll take your skills elsewhere is more likely to provoke hostility than to make a persuasive case for a raise.

N o matter how good your current job is, no matter how much you are earning, and no matter how stimulating the conversation is at the water cooler, one day you will come to work, look around, and decide that it's time for a new job.

Should you tell your manager you're looking?

No.

Coming into your manager's office with a solid offer from another company and using it to negotiate a raise and/or promotion is good strategy. But any experienced programmer—indeed, anyone who has spent several years building a career—knows that meeting your manager armed with nothing but the threat (however subtle) that you'll take your skills elsewhere is more likely to provoke hostility than to make a persuasive case for a raise. This seems obvious, but younger programmers may not know or have enough social savvy to understand all the issues involved; the question warrants a chapter in this book because I've been asked to answer it so many times over my career.

My forty years of observing corporate programmers solicit and receive raises and promotions—or jump ship for a really big raise—have led me to form two strategies that bear on this. They apply across the breadth of programming, both in technical issues and in interpersonal issues. I'll share both with you in this chapter.

Get the Lay of the Land

Analyze your boss. If he has been in the same management job for many years, he is probably set in his ways, and may have little ambition to move up. In that case, don't assume that your boss has a plan for his programmers to move up either. Such a long-term boss is likely to hope that his programmers stay in their jobs and provide stability to the department. On the other hand, a newly promoted programming manager is probably still flushed with the excitement of his promotion and expanded responsibilities, and may very well be receptive to and supportive of his programmers when they show ambition.

Analyze the careers of previous programmers in your company. If the job track record is up rather than out, you have excellent prospects to move up in your company. However, if the last ten corporate programmers have opted out of the company rather than up for their next job, you might want to focus on that prospect also. The human resources department should be picking up on that expensive trend for your company and inquiring about it, but sometimes it doesn't.

Outflank Your Manager

It's a fundamental theory of war: Never attack an enemy who has dug into a defensive position. Instead, come up with a strategy to outflank him. Triumphant outflankings are the thrilling bits in the history books: Hannibal crossing the Alps, Stonewall Jackson's Second Corps routing the Union right at Chancellorsville, the Germans outflanking the Maginot fortifications...

Your enemy is the IT department's budget, which you have, no doubt, been told is unyielding. Your job is to get more of that budget devoted to you. But you don't attack directly by going into your boss's office and telling him you're looking around for another job. You study the terrain and come up with a flanking maneuver. You've observed your boss; you've observed the careers of those who came before you. Now you know the lay of the land. Your next step is to make your flanking movement.

On a piece of paper, list the positive and negative things about your current job, including your relationships with your manager and your peers. Review each one of them, and see if you can develop a strategy that will improve the negatives. For instance, if your manager has no formal, written, significant educational plan for you to keep current or advance to a higher position, then you must ask for one.

Ask for a meeting with your manager and say, courteously, that you are ambitious and have proved yourself to be capable, productive, and loyal, and that you want his or her help, guidance, and counsel on how to move up in the company.

You can judge from your manager's reaction and subsequent actions whether this in-company approach will be successful. If your manager is not proactive in helping you, ask him or her to search for another IT manager or project team that might accommodate your ambitions.

If your immediate manager won't or can't help you and you have the requisite ambition, then you can ask for a meeting with your manager's manager to voice your desires, which are to move up in compensation and title and responsibility within your current company. If your manager cannot help you, then he knows that you will eventually leave, so he has (or should have) a real interest in protecting himself from the inevitable questions about why one of his key people left the company. That means your manager should actually encourage your meeting with his manager (especially if you have been calm, polite, and sincere), and perhaps set it up, so you can express your needs and desires to executive management.

If you are a reasonably good, productive, and loyal programmer, then your leaving the company will cost it many thousands of dollars in cost of expertise. The IT executive is likely to make a considered evaluation of this and somehow find a way to accommodate such an ambitious and serious programmer. No one, particularly your manager, should fault you for trying to move up within the system. That you have to initiate that upward movement yourself may be surprising and disconcerting, but at least you done everything you could to rise within the company.

$$ The Bottom Line $$

Often, the best opportunities are had within your own company. When you are looking for new challenges, scope out your present stomping grounds first. What you observe and what you learn can give you a good idea whether your future is right in front of you.

If you choose to interview at another company, ask for what you want, not what you think you are worth or what you think the company is willing to pay. You may have to accept less that you wanted, but at least you had the courage to ask for it. And you may well be surprised and get what you asked for. At least your new company will know that you have confidence in yourself.

CHAPTER TWENTY SIX

A Big Push Out of the House

You know that you need to leave. Perhaps you've even found a job. At this point, many experienced programmers still ask how they should go out the door. My answer is simple—leave them smiling.

S ometimes, in spite of your research within your own company, you can't find new opportunities and challenges. You're stuck. You're bored. You know the grass is greener on the other side of the computer monitor, but you can't quite get yourself motivated to really assess your situation. And so...you do nothing.

Well, while you let moss grow under your keyboard, consider that someone else might also be watching your career and assessing whether you are still a vital member of the team. In other words, while you're thinking you're stuck, someone else might be thinking that you're done, in a very big way.

What can you do about these types of situations? This chapter gives you tips about how to detect shifting winds and, more important, how to leave when the time comes.

How to Know When It's Time to Leave

This list is a mere sampling of the potential clues that it's time to consider moving on, or even that someone else is considering a job termination for you:

- You have lots of time and energy to chitchat, doodle, surf the Web, and get coffee. You have to ask yourself, "What can I do today to look busy?"

- Your job doesn't require you to learn anything new, and you are not learning anything new on your own.

- You have been in the same job with the same responsibilities for several years, and it has become routine—even boring.

- You are uneasy with new technology that might improve your productivity.

- There is no funding in your department for education in new technology, and no management awareness of the need to implement current IT technology.

- Others are being recognized and promoted—or leaving for better jobs—and you are not.

- Your company is getting smaller and less profitable.

- Corporate direction changes to another focus and away from your skills.

- Your manager seems strangely aloof to you, but not to others.

- Your job evaluations are going down, you're not getting significant raises, and your manager doesn't have a plan to help you.

- Your boss never asks, "What are you working on?"

- Nothing ever goes wrong.

- Your company is bought.

- You are switched to a team or applications or a manager that you can't stand.

- You think you can do this job for the rest of your career with no sweat.

- They move you to the bullpen from your own office.

Do you see yourself in any of these items? You may be in line for a premature exit. Be prepared. Start networking and polishing up your skills now. You are just a short time away from some serious job searching.

How to Plan Your Leaving

You know that you need to leave. Perhaps you've even found a job. At this point, many experienced programmers still ask how they should go out the door. With notice? With no notice? My answer is simple—it depends on your company's policy. But no matter what, leave them smiling when you go out that door.

Observe what normally happens when employees leave. If they normally stay for two or three weeks after they give notice, you also will probably be expected to give such a notice, unless you are leaving under quite nasty circumstances. You will find that doing two or three more weeks of productive work as you exit a company is quite easy, even if you don't particularly like your manager or your job.

On the other hand, the policy of your company may be to have you escorted out immediately after you've given notice (not what anyone would consider an enlightened policy, especially when security escorts the person out). If that's the policy, you will, of course, hold your counsel about leaving until the day you plan to depart.

How to Behave on Your Way Out the Door

Your company's exit interview, if there is one, is another test of your ability to maintain your calm and perspective. A company may utilize the formal Human Resources exit interview to obtain helpful information and to gauge your state of mind as you leave. Human Resources will most probably focus on management and compensation issues. You should be guardedly candid if pressed, but not cruel to your manager. HR uses compensation feedback to keep the company's hiring and compensation packages competitive so that the company will not lose more good employees like you.

Any way you leave—voluntarily, terminated, or retired—you are going through a transition period that taxes your perspective and perhaps your fairness.

You can turn an exit interview to everyone's advantage if you just try to be as fair and as objective as you can be. This is not the time for trashing former managers and co-workers. It is the time for objectivity and professionalism.

$$ The Bottom Line $$

Sometimes, whether you like it or not, the winds of your career will shift and you will find yourself subtly or not-so-subtly pushed out the door, either by circumstances or by your lack of current skills. If you find yourself in the checklist in this chapter, watch out. You're on your way out—in a hurry.

Whether you leave voluntarily or involuntarily, be civil; leave with grace. At some point, someone will surely be inquiring about your job history to the Human Resources Department or to a previous manager of yours, even if you don't ask them for job references.

Section 4

~

Beyond Programming

Advice for Would-Be Managers, Programming Consultants, Software Developers, and Business Owners

CHAPTER TWENTY SEVEN

Jumping to Management

Each step upward into management requires the programmer to program less, to understand more about the company business processes and staff, and to depend on communication skills while letting others do the detailed work. Each step takes a manager farther away from the objectivity and solitude of programming toward the more subjective and political environment of management.

Like me, many programmers find a career as a head-down code writer (pure programmer) both challenging and fulfilling. But some programmers suspect, when they've been on the job for a while, that they have more of an affinity for IT management than for coding.

If that has been your discovery, you haven't wasted your time by entering through the programming door: Your skills and experience as a programmer are splendid grounding for a career as an IT manager.

You'll find that each step upward into management requires the programmer to program less, to understand more about the company business processes and staff, and to depend on communication skills while letting others do the detailed work. Each step takes a manager farther away from the objectivity and solitude of programming toward the more subjective and political environment of management.

This chapter offers the stories of two programmers who reinvented themselves as managers.

Reinvention 1:
From Programmer to Director of Systems Analysis

The frequently followed path upward goes from corporate programmer to systems analyst to project leader to programming manager to IT manager to CIO (Chief Information Officer) to VP of Information Technology. Joe Cohill, Director of Business Analysis at a multi-billion-dollar manufacturing company outside Philadelphia, followed a slightly different route—from public accountant to programmer to systems analyst to project leader to divisional manager to corporate management.

What got Joe into management was a combination of qualities that every manager must have: business understanding, communications skills, the ability to lead, and that frequently touted virtue, "people skills." Which include, Joe says, "being able to take the project by the horns calmly, not getting flustered, and getting the job done without pointing fingers."

Joe got a public accounting degree from the Philadelphia Institute of Textiles and Sciences; he went into accounting because his father was a CPA. In the late 1980s, as he looked around the small packaging company where he'd landed after working with his father for several years, Joe observed that "people were relying on programmers to get things done. The accounting department was considered a necessary evil, but the company really needed these programming guys."

So Joe asked if he could switch into the IT department, took a course in programming at a local community college, and learned on the job (with the help of a guided-learning tape from IBM). "And people were nice enough to mentor me," Joe says.

Working in so small a company gave Joe an incredible learning opportunity. He got to be everything—analyst, programmer, tester, implementer, and trainer; he met the worker on the factory floor, the middle manager, and the end user. All of this, plus his experience with RF (Radio Frequency) barcode scanning and data collection, got him a systems analysis job (with salary increase) at a company five times larger than his old firm.

He no longer did programming. At the new job, he was an integral part of a team that immediately began automating the company warehouse, using a sophisticated, complex software package (until then, the company had only in-house-written code). Just knowing how to install that package greatly increased his market value. "For the first couple of months, there were rough spots," he acknowledges. "It's a difficult thing to change the company culture. But once we'd worked through it all, it was a successful template for all the other warehouses the company acquired [there are now seven]."

Working with the engineering department and distribution management made Joe more visible—and promotable. Now, after two promotions, he's part of a three-member management team that analyzes business processes throughout the company. Joe uses his programming, hardware, and project leadership knowledge to help the other divisions in his company meet their financial goals.

Reinvention 2:
From Programmer to Vice-President of Operations

Harry Ciaccio is Vice-President of Operations for a large manufacturing and distribution company in suburban Philadelphia. He started as a programmer, but after a few years he decided to focus on the operations side of the business.

"I like to program," he says, "but I fell in love with manufacturing. The advantage you have when you enter a company through the information technology side," Harry says, "is that you get involved in every aspect of the business. As you study the company's operations, you interact with the managers of every department—manufacturing, finance, distribution, customer service—and with the chief financial officer and the chief executive officer as well. You are right in front of them in terms of opportunity."

Harry should know: He entered the business world as a programmer, and programming set him on the pathway to management. Now he's an executive for an apparel firm that buys its materials and sells its products throughout the world. "We have our own cut-and-sew operation in the Dominican Republic. We also utilize more than fifty contractors throughout the world, along with distribution centers in South Carolina, Florida, and California," he says. "We have a buying office overseas, so our supply chain logistics are very complex."

Harry oversees the work of many departments: purchasing, production planning, customer service, information technology, and some aspects of warehousing and distribution. "Basically," he says, "I oversee all of the company's day-to-day operations."

Harry says he wouldn't change a single thing about his career path. "It had two parts," he says. "One was the technical part, where I really wanted to excel in understanding computer hardware and the programming languages. When I got my first job—for a computer peripheral manufacturer, back in 1973—I wrote in RPG, Assembler, and COBOL. These three languages gave me a broad-based knowledge and allowed me to work with many different computers. I wanted to be the best programmer the company would ever have. I don't want to sound pompous, but I believe I accomplished that goal.

"However, the other part of my career was to learn the business functions. When I started, I was doing computer operations and programming. I didn't have a clue as to how the people in the accounting and manufacturing departments went about doing whatever they did. I then realized that just being a computer whiz was not enough. I had to be on a level playing field with middle and upper management."

Accordingly, Harry went out and took several night courses at a local college in business and management. "The more I got involved in systems development and programming, the more business aspects I began to learn," he says. "For instance, when I was at my second job, I worked with the controller, and we developed financial budgets, enhanced the accounts payable system, and developed a cost accounting (work order management) system. That's how I learned debits and credits.

"But what really changed my direction was when I worked on my first MRP [Manufacturing Resource Planning] project. I got deeply involved with all aspects of manufacturing from master scheduling to shop floor control. It was at this point in my career that I decided to get more involved with business and less involved with being a good programmer."

Harry saw his opportunity and seized it. He left his first job and went to work for an apparel company that was struggling to get its technology systems going. He told the principal of the company that he was not interested in being just a technical person. Harry said, "I'd love to help you with your technical problems, but really, from a career standpoint I would want the opportunity to manage the manufacturing operation." The principal of the company said, "Look, you solve our technology problems and when something comes up in manufacturing I'll give you a shot at it," Harry says.

"That's all I had to hear. That's the change I wanted to make. I loved computers, but I loved the broader business aspect—what computers could do to increase productivity and improve the bottom line. I felt that with what I knew about technology and what I knew about business, I could help any company grow and become more profitable. In fact, that's exactly what happened. So, coming up as a programmer and doing systems analysis and systems design was my springboard to getting into top management."

$$ The Bottom Line $$

If you find that you have a bent for management, go for it. Your programming skills will add to your luster as a manager. To move up, throw yourself into every sort of task, and try become known to managers and engineers in other divisions, as Joe Cohill did. In addition, take courses in business and management, as Harry Ciaccio did. It is these types of activities that can lead to a lasting career in management.

CHAPTER TWENTY EIGHT

The Top of the Pyramid:
The Programmer Consultant

Part-time consulting is the very best way to test and validate your ability to make the significant leap from sheltered employee programmer into the "top pay for outstanding performance every day" world of the independent programmer consultant. Are you good enough to be a consultant?

An independent programmer consultant (programmer contractor) is an entrepreneur who does programming or related work—not as a company employee, but for a per-hour or per-day fee (or, infrequently, for a project fee). He must get the work, perform it, manage the client, invoice the client, secure payment, pay all taxes (taxes are not withheld from the checks he receives for his services), and meet all federal, state, and local reporting requirements. An experienced independent programmer commands top dollar—probably $75 to $125 per hour in the United States.

Consultants are paid so well because they are the emergency-room physicians of the information technology world. They are expected to perform miracles—and often do. They are the programmers in any department who are under the greatest pressure; they feel the highest level of stress (see Chapter 12 "Mission: Impossible"), for by the time they are called in, disaster is usually imminent. I have arrived at companies and found the CIO—once, even the CEO—literally waiting at the door for me to immediately resolve critical business problems.

On one of my consulting assignments, the president of a major company and I were shaking hands to cement our relationship (he had just hired me under my normal consultant conditions—a handshake, rather than a formal written contract). Suddenly, he said, ruefully, "But you'll be making more than any of my employees!"

Right—and rightly so! Any programmer called in to be a consultant must have impressive skills in coding, business savvy, and risk management, and he must be willing to take on the toughest, most high-visibility projects.

"The budgeting for an in-house programmer in my area—Philadelphia—might be around $74,000 a year, but for a consultant programmer it would be $150,000," says Dennis Mulcare, who spent twenty years becoming experienced and well-rounded as a pure programmer, designer of operating systems, IBM systems engineer, IBM computer salesman, and vice-president of marketing for a software development company before venturing out as a top programming consultant.

Sam Gottlieb, the former technical interviewer who is now a consulting programmer, notes, "I still remember when I made the move from my in-house job to my first consulting position. I had three years under my belt. When I became a consultant, my income nearly doubled."

The Brokered Programming Consultant

A "brokered" programmer consultant works for a company offering programmer consulting services—typically, a consulting firm, an accounting company, a hardware company, or a software vendor. These "brokers" (consulting-services firms) send programmers (who are either their employees or independent consultants) to their client companies to do expert work. These programmers are usually very well trained and experienced. And, because the broker company finds the client, manages the client, invoices the client, and secures payment for the service, these programmers can spend all their energy focusing on the actual programming work.

The broker may charge $200 to more than $300 an hour for the services of the programmers it sends out to its client companies. What do the programmers get? The independent consultants sent out by the broker may be billing the broker $100 to $160 an hour for their services—and therefore they pay the broker a premium of 25 to 30 percent of the billing rate for finding the work and doing the billing. But if the programmer sent out by the broker is on the broker's payroll as an employee, he may be getting a mere $40 per hour as a salary.

Naturally, the question "Why should I get paid $40 an hour for my work when my employer bills the client at $200 an hour?" crosses the minds of many employees of the brokering company. That nagging question becomes more insistent when, say, the manager of a client company at which the brokered programmer has performed admirably solicits him to work independently for $100 per hour—a big raise for the programmer, but only half of what the client is paying the broker for that programmer's services.

The answer to this question is, once again, "Everything is economic."

In good economic times, employees shift into consulting—either as independent contractors or as consultants sent out by brokers. In bad economic times, expert programmers shift from consultancy to the shelter of an employer; the consultant opts for a weekly paycheck. The good news for consultants is that their superior skills and savvy make them coveted employee programmers during the bad times.

What to Consider Before Venturing Out

You may choose to leave your salaried job as an employee programmer to become a full-time independent contractor. Or, like most consultants, you may dip your toes into the independent-consulting world part-time, while retaining your security as an employee. Part-time programmer consulting is the very best way to test and validate your skills and ability to make the significant leap from sheltered employee programmer into the "top pay for outstanding performance every day" world of the independent programmer consultant.

As an independent consultant, you'll get to select the major projects that interest you and that showcase your ability and enhance your reputation and marketability. That's a heady freedom not available to the company employee. And as a consultant you're spared being immersed in company politics.

Of course, you must weigh consultants' high compensation (often $4,000 per week or more) against the knowledge that consultants may not work a steady fifty-two weeks a year. However, not having to work fifty-two weeks a year is why some people become consultants in the first place.

Independent programmer consultants get to negotiate every aspect of their working conditions with their client company. A major condition often is working only four days a week (like many doctors) of nine or ten billable hours per day, or working remotely (at home) on big projects, and taking several weeks off between projects.

Wise consultants like to be working with more than one client company at any time. (That way, they'll have projects when a major client has nothing for them to do.) And juggling clients increases the billable rate (everything is economic). You can get the rate that the highest client company pays when there is more work than they can handle.

I went to Australia on a three-week vacation with my wife and daughter after completing a major project for a client company for whom I consulted virtually full-time for five years. Then I spent some time in Australia working with another client company before returning, refreshed, to begin my next exciting major project with my old client without having any lingering responsibilities for my previous projects. Company employees rarely get a real reprieve from work, since when they return from time off they have to take care of the work that has piled up while they were away.

There's another financial reality to consider: Because the consultant is an independent contractor, he has to pay the employer's share of FICA (payroll) taxes as well as his own. A salaried employee now pays 7.5 percent in FICA taxes, the consultant pays 15 percent. The independent consultant is paid only for services rendered, with no vacation, holiday, personal days paid, and with no health coverage.

Another consideration: If your consulting job isn't within commuting distance, you'll have hotel and restaurant expenses (though they're tax deductible). However, consultants can often negotiate reasonable travel and living expenses to be paid by the client (travel expenses to and from the client company being from your office, which is typically in your basement).

A warning to programmer consultants: Invoice your client company regularly (and promptly) for billable services, and provide a detailed one-page summary of your accomplishments each week. Specify payment terms with your client and then insist on payment within that time. One independent consultant I know allowed $11,000 of billable work to accumulate—and got none of it because the client company went into bankruptcy proceedings.

The Programmer Consultant Environment

A successful independent programmer consultant needs all the skills of an employee programmer plus those of an entrepreneur. Here are some of the rewards and requirements of this "top of the programming pyramid" work:

- The money—You can make double that of a top employee programmer.
- Independence—You are your own boss.
- Variety—You select the work that you want and like.
- Challenge—You get the best (the most visible and exciting) projects.
- Project orientation—Every consulting job is a project.
- Entrepreneurship—You may be your entire company.
- Work hours—You negotiate when and where you will work.
- Personal time—You can take off twelve weeks and make more that year than employee programmers.
- Reputation—You are recognized and sought after by top management at multiple client companies.
- Skills inventory—You must demonstrate superior skills.
- Flexibility—You can and should have several concurrent client corporations bidding for your services.
- Instant goodbye—You have the power take leave of a client instantly to move on to another.
- Additional work—You can be an expert witness, or move to management jobs or a top IT management job.

- Wide network—You typically have a large network of clients and other IT professionals
- Work from home—Big projects may allow you to work from your deck at home
- Management skills—You need to become an effective manager while consulting
- Negotiating skills—You get to negotiate everything
- Direct feedback—You get paid or get asked to leave based on your managers' perception of your performance
- Consultant contract—I like the handshake agreement
- Leadership—A consultant programmer is a leader

How Good Are You?

Before you begin to consider whether you can afford to leave your job and live without a salary, take an unvarnished look at your programming skills and the additional skills you'll need to be a successful programming consultant.

A successful independent or brokered programmer consultant has all the skills of an employee programmer and the skills of an entrepreneur. You need to be a quick study.

> "As a consultant you can be thrown into a different industry every week, and you have to be able to jump in there and learn what they really want, knowing that you have this programming skill and you can make things happen on a computer," Dennis Mulcare says. "You could be doing accounting, like general ledger work, or it could be trying to automate a warehouse so that when the packages come down the line they get put into the right shopping trucks, or that when a customer's order comes into the warehouse they can find the size item they want. How do you program that?"

> Dennis's experience as a multi-dimensional player in the world of information technology made him the quick study he is. His various jobs (programmer, systems analyst, salesman, marketer) got him out of his company's office and into the laboratories, factory floors, and offices of many clients. That not only gave him the experience that turned him into an expert, but gave him a working relationship with a series of IT directors who knew his work and might hire him as a consultant.

"There are people who don't like to visit with people too much, and want to just have the problem to solve on the computer," Dennis says. These are not people who should consider a consulting career. When I was an IBM systems engineer, then an IBM salesman, and then a vice-president of marketing for a software development company, the job was to go out to a customer, find out what he wanted, and see if your computer or your custom program or your software package could meet his needs.

"As a systems engineer at IBM, that's what I did. I'd go out to the non-technical world, find a requirement, then come back and see how I could solve it. Maybe I'd need to bring a package in and modify it, or do some programming in a new area. Maybe I could solve the program through hardware technology. I've been up against everything from automating laboratories to automating shop floors, where I was trying to track production going through a plant or warehouses and finding out where I'd need to bar-code things.

"My bent—the best thing that I can offer now—is working with people to find out what the company's requirements are, and then bringing those requirements back into the technical work I do. It's developing the business solutions that is my real expertise." (Heard that theme before? It'll need to be yours too.)

Who Will Hire You?

How do you acquire clients? The answer is surprisingly simple: You ask to be a consulting programmer—perhaps starting part-time as a second job—or you put yourself in a position to be asked to be a consulting programmer.

My own introduction into the world of IT consulting came, perhaps unbelievably, when I had only six months of IT experience and before I was a permanent employee programmer of any company. I was asked by IT management of a major oil company if I would please work as a (highly paid) consultant for them during my spare time in my last six months of school before graduation from Drexel Institute of Technology (now Drexel University).

I was working for IBM as a temporary employee with the title of systems-engineer trainee; this was my last six-month industry cooperative education at Drexel. During my six months at IBM I had attended customer-education classes to learn how to "program" (wire the control panels) of the then-prevalent IBM unit record punched card machines that produced IT reports. Then I was sent out into major companies to "program" (wire the control panels of) the IBM machines in their IT data centers.

I knew immediately that I was good at doing that job. I was a very enthusiastic—and, apparently, a very hard and productive—worker, because near the end of my IBM co-op experience, Jack Higby, the IT manager of a major oil company, asked me to continue to work for them as an IT consultant whenever I could spare time from school.

The Drexel cooperative industry program allowed students to pay their way through a five-year program by earning money in industry during their education, and now I could earn top money as an IT consultant during my school sessions rather than take a low-paying part-time job. Doing this work solidified my chances at a programming career after graduation. I took only one job interview at graduation—IBM.

IBM had trained me and put me in a position to be solicited to be a highly paid consultant by a major company. All I had to do was perform, and take the plunge into consulting when asked.

You can find programmer consulting opportunities by doing exactly the same things that consultants like Sam Gottlieb and Dennis Muclare have done. First, hone your programming skills. Next, position yourself to be considered for consulting jobs. The major corporations and the consulting companies that provide programming consultants have a constant need to fill their consultant programmer positions. Become expert in the software application niche of major companies, and then solicit them for a consulting job.

Most employee programmers that I know have never queried a consulting company or employment agency for a possible consulting job, and yet they wonder just how it is that programmer consultants are born.

Dennis Mulcare notes: "I sell myself to customers to do jobs, work through the jobs, and then try to find new jobs within that company. I've been with the same client for three and a half years. Typically, you work for a client for about six months. But I was always able to do the job and then find somebody else in the company that wanted my help, based on my success.

"As I moved in my career from being a programmer with a company to being a systems engineer with IBM, and then a salesman at IBM, I was more independent with each step," Dennis Mulcare says. *"And I also had more risk with each step. But with more risk came more reward. Now, as a consultant, I have the greatest rewards. Certainly the risk is there, too, but because of the current market for mainframe programmers, at the moment there's not much risk.*

"It's really exciting when you can sit down with somebody in the very raw state of understanding and find out what this person's business is and be able to come back and manufacture a solution. It's very gratifying—gratifying on different levels. It's gratifying on the level of putting together a solution and planning it out, and it's gratifying taking pieces of the solution and programming them and having the program work and do the right thing.

"When you sit down at the customer's office when it's finally delivered and you see that the people in the different departments that are using your product really feel that they're saving time and being more efficient, and they say things like 'This job I just did in two minutes—this would have taken me a week without the computer'—that's the kind of thing that really makes you feel good."

$$ THE BOTTOM LINE $$

Successful independent consultants reap the highest compensation a programmer can hope for (unless he invents, and owns the copyright to, some major piece of software). But high pay is just one of the consultant's rewards. If you venture out on your own, you'll be your own boss. You'll take on only the work you want and like. You'll be recognized as an expert who can handle the most visible, challenging, exciting projects.

CHAPTER TWENTY NINE

Write for Your Industry

If you write code for a living and have a good idea that you're eager to communicate to your peers, you have a shot at getting published in a prestigious information technology magazine, on an important information technology Web site, or in a technical book. And, most agreeably, your name will be on what you write.

The superior work you do as a corporate programmer—writing code elegantly, say, or finding creative solutions to your company's problems—will bring you no widespread prestige. What you produce, year after year, will be invisible to everyone except the programmers who review and maintain your programs. That is the deal you made when you took the job.

And yet, your experience and talent may have led you to create an important programming technique, or you may have acquired so much expertise in a certain field, that you deserve a forum in which you can articulate your strong opinions on controversial programming issues.

Happily, it's not hard to break the bonds of anonymity. If you write code for a living and have a good idea that you're eager to communicate to your peers, you (yes, *you*) have a very strong shot at getting published in a prestigious information technology magazine, on an important Information Technology Web site, or in a technical book that sells for $100 or more. And, most agreeably, your name will be on what you write.

Fame, if Not Fortune

Getting published may or may not bring you what you consider a worthwhile article fee; it may not yield significant book royalties. But it will add an impressive credential to your résumé, build your reputation as an expert, lay your passionately held conviction about some IT issue before thousands of your peers—and boost your ego. (There is something highly satisfying about turning the pages of a handsomely designed, influential IT magazine and coming upon your article. The psychic reward will probably be just as strong a year later, when, on rereading your piece, you still find your argument persuasive—even powerful.)

"Time and time again I've seen a programmer become something of a name, based on his writing," notes Merrikay Lee, president of MC Press (the publisher of this book). "The path usually starts with the writer's submitting tips/techniques (300 to 800 words) to magazines. Often the writer doesn't get paid for them, or the payment is just a pittance. But if the tips/techniques are good, they will get the attention of an editor.

"That often leads to writing articles for a magazine. The going rate at MC Press Online (which publishes *MCMagOnline* and *MC RPG Developer*) is about 20 cents a word, although that certainly varies from publication to publication. Once a writer has proved that he can write and that he has important information to share, a book is a natural follow-on."

Asked about royalties, Merrikay says, "They vary. A would-be author, in my opinion, should take on a book project for the prestige and career-building opportunities rather than for the royalty money. A frank discussion with the publisher after a book proposal has been made will usually give the author a good idea of what kind of royalties can be expected.

"But the additional perks can be substantial. Sometimes, publishing articles can lead to speaking engagements at technical conferences or seminars. It also can turn into consulting engagements that can be very lucrative. Perhaps the best way to think about it is that a book can turn a programmer into the recognized expert in his or her field. Where he takes that advantage is up to him."

Finding the Market Is Easy

Breaking into IT publishing is relatively easy. I should know. I was never a star in English class, and yet, after many decades as a programmer I have suddenly become, within the last five years, the author of six published articles and a soon-to-be-published book.

I've found that publishers of information technology books and magazines normally respond promptly and courteously to their writers' submissions. (That, at least, has been my experience.) General-interest publishers are swamped with unwanted submissions. But IT publishers aren't dodging writers—they're trolling for them. They really want and need to hear from you.

IT publishers welcome potential writers at their Web sites with statements encouraging submissions, and even with detailed guidelines on what makes a good article and how to submit your idea. For example, take a look at the Web site of MC Press (*www.mcpressonline.com*). Also review other IT magazines that you should find in the IT reference library of your company or at your bookstore or library. Review the Web site of *iSeries NEWS* magazine (*www.iseriesnetwork.com/info/networkpubs*) or *e-Pro Magazine* (*www.e-promag.com/epinfo/write*). You can get information on writing for *Oracle* and *Profit* magazines by visiting *www.oracle.com/oramag*; on writing for *Linux Journal* by visiting *www.linuxjournal.com*; on writing for *Java Developer's Journal* by visiting *www.sys-con.com/java/authors/index.cfm*. These are just examples: Pick an IT magazine you read and go to its Web site; you're likely to find a "we'd like to hear from new writers" welcome there.

Working IT professionals form the talent pool from which IT magazines draw their writers. After all, who is likely to have better credentials for spotting problems and coming up with solutions than the programmers and managers who deal with them every day?

Shaping Your Ideas Is the Next Step

So, how do you develop your thoughts into an article idea? Often, a good magazine piece starts taking form in your brain because something about your work chronically irritates you. You may notice, in going from shop to shop, that programmers (or managers) consistently do something the hard, ignorant way. "Why don't they do it this way?" you keep asking yourself as you do the same task, using a simple alternative technique that you've come up with.

That's just the kind of "Aha!" moment that you can turn into the springboard for an article query to the editor of an IT magazine. If the problem that your solution remedies is significant enough and widespread enough, an IT-journal editor is likely to welcome a query from you about it.

Maybe you'd want to do a short article—an 800-word single-page article or a 1,000- to 1,500-word case study. Maybe you'd need the 2,000 to 3,000 words of a feature article to get your thoughts across. Your editor will tell you how long he or she thinks the article should be. You can recognize and adopt the tone and approach of the current writers in the magazine (this is most likely to get your article accepted, because it shows you the style that the editors like), or you can use your own style and approach to effectively communicate your message.

My First Sale

Here's how I got my first article published. I've set down the process because it may give you some idea how a compelling thought can be refined into an article idea.

As I've noted above, a writer needs no inside track to get a response from editors in the IT field. For my first article assignment, though, I did have an inside track, since Debbie, my sister, was an editor at a new, limited-circulation magazine, *NYCitylife*. I had an idea for the magazine's special section on "changing one's life in mid-career."

I believed that programming would make a good second career, especially if the applicant had a business background. In that spring of 1998, jobs were plentiful—indeed, corporations' appetite for programmers, especially legacy-code programmers, was so ravenous that companies were luring workers out of retirement to get America's business and government computers ready for the start of Year 2000.

But where were all the applicants? I surmised that people were still staying away in droves because they believe the stereotype that programming is dull work. I also wanted to get the word out that English and history majors, despite their dislike of math, can become splendid programmers. So I wrote a short proposal (one and a half pages) to the *NYCitylife* editor-in-chief, asking her to let me make my case ("programming is a terrific, creative career") to the readers of the magazine. I got the assignment. Writing the piece was easy. I just had to pour my thoughts into the computer; after all, I'd been obsessing on this very subject for many months.

My First IT Magazine Sale

My first article for an IT Magazine ("Building a Better Programmer," for *Midrange Computing*, the print magazine that was the predecessor for the current online publication *MCMagOnline*) was prompted by my visit to the company's Web site to look for books or other interesting topics I could review online. My eye fell on a button that said "Article Opportunities." On my click I found a Web page from the acquisitions editor, encouraging the submission of articles— apparently from even people like me who were without extensive previous published works.

I popped off a list of ten article ideas to her.

That acquisitions editor promptly responded (picking what I thought was my eighth-most-interesting idea). It was easy to write (because it was about giving programmers the private office space and quiet I believe they need—a subject you will now recognize as one of my obsessions). Once it went to print, I was now a published author in a respected IT magazine. I'd gotten paid for the article ($500). I'd gotten lots of "attaboys" from my colleagues and nice e-mails from readers. I even had the pleasure of knowing that my readers shared my zeal—several of them wrote that they had left a copy of my article on their manager's office chair.

After the Article Is Published

Once your idea becomes your first well-received article in a national magazine, you have an open door for other articles, and now you have a good chance to get a book published.

After writing a few articles, I found that the brevity and conciseness that are the mantra for magazine articles left too much of what I thought was important material on the magazine's cutting-room floor. Discovering that I had ideas and opinions for dozens of related articles that I wanted to explore much more fully made writing books my next logical choice.

$$ The Bottom Line $$

Break out of the darkness into the light. Query a technical editor and get your name in print. Holding your book or magazine article in your hands is a tangible reward—a reward most people never get on the job. In addition, a published article can lead to other opportunities, since it builds your name and reputation within the IT field.

CHAPTER THIRTY

Founding and Running Your Own Firm

The hazards of founding your own firm include serious financial risk and grueling, anxious hours at the office. But there's great reward in seeing a company you've created take hold, and then thrive. For entrepreneurs with the right idea and the courage and energy to bring it to fruition, becoming the successful founder of a company is a very possible dream.

Gene Bonett, the exuberant entrepreneur whose programming philosophy—*you've got to know the territory*—leads off this book, founded his own firm when he was forty-five. Like many programmers who leave the security of an IT staff job to become entrepreneurs, he was taking quite a flyer. He had family responsibilities (a wife and two daughters), his move meant a $40,000 pay cut, and he had no nest egg to live on.

Fortunately, Gene had no idea what pitfalls lie in the path of the entrepreneur. And his risk-taking turned out well—as risk-taking sometimes does. His advice to new entrepreneurs? Don't do it his way.

The Struggle to Survive Was Brutal

"The programming I did on my way up isn't what gives me my personal satisfaction," says Gene Bonett, founder, president, and CEO of Xperia, a software development and consulting firm in Allentown, Pennsylvania. "My personal satisfaction comes from being someone who started a software development company that now employs 42 people.

"It's fulfilling to fly to Europe to visit our clients. I get a lot of satisfaction out of having owners of major companies call me and say, 'We think your software is top shelf.' I like knowing that the packages we've created have helped a lot of companies understand what MIS and IT are all about."

Though he likes where he is today, Gene acknowledges that the struggle to survive as a business owner was "brutal—if I'd known what I was in for, I never would have gotten started," he says. But since his incorporation day, Gene has shepherded his firm's software—which targets the apparel and footwear industries-—from green-screen on the mainframe to business-to-business applications on the midrange computer, using IBM's WebSphere product.

There's a Crossroads in Everyone's Career

Before he took his flyer into entrepreneurship, Gene followed the long, slow path upward that was the typical lot of the first-generation programmer. A three-month stint in Vietnam as a 24-year-old Marine led him to the conclusion "Boy, this is not for me." Since he didn't know what *was* for him, he took an aptitude test. It showed that he had a bent for computer work and programming, so he spent two years at Pierce Junior College studying computer science.

That was Gene's first crossroads—finding a general direction for a career. His first job was close to the bottom—as a computer operator running batch programs (working with keypunch-card readers, loading cards, and changing tapes) at a wedding-gown manufacturing company in Philadelphia. "The only people lower than the operators were the keypunchers," he says. The moving-up pace was glacial in those days. After he'd been at the company five or six years, the MIS director left, and Gene got his post. Still, it was considered a leap. "I asked for the MIS job," Gene says. "In fact, I told them I'd leave if I didn't get it. You have to decide when your opportunity is there. The MIS director said, 'You think you can do it?' and I said, 'Absolutely.' And I spent a lot of time trying to learn how to do it."

He had made his way upward from operator to head of the company's computer operations department, taking courses at night at Temple University and Drexel Institute of Technology (now Drexel

University) in his quest to get into programming. He wrote programs on the side while doing his operator's job, and lurked around the IBM systems engineers working there (Garry Reinhard and me), asking for enlightenment about the computers we were installing.

"Now, when I took over for the MIS director, I didn't get much time to get into the technical side of the business—the programming side," Gene says. "There was more time to learn the applications system side." And that turned out to be fortunate, for Gene found that he liked the system side better. "The system side is learning the business, generating and developing systems to support the company's growth. That job is what they now call the CIO.

"I got where I got because I had a goal. I quickly realized that people on the business side made more money than the technically oriented people. You've got to learn as much as you can about a company, its systems, its computers, the programming aspect of it.

"There's a crossroads in everyone's career. You either want to go very heavily into a technical environment where you're programming, understanding the capabilities of machines from a technical perspective, or you go off and become a manager or information officer (CIO).

"Do you want to be technically oriented or business oriented? I took the approach that being more business oriented is going to further my career faster and get me where I wanted to be—which at that point was a MIS director who really understood the apparel industry. That was my goal, and I spent a lot of time trying to reach it."

I Had to Get Out

After Gene had worked there for ten years, he switched to another company, which was a large men's-tailored-clothing company. "It was a very real challenge for me," he says, "because I was used to the job I had had for ten years. I knew that company from the inside out, because I'd come up from the operations aspect of that business. I thought I was a good IT director there, but could I duplicate that in another company where I hadn't started at the bottom?

"It turned out that I could. I started as MIS director, with thirty-five people to manage. We needed to develop systems quickly. It was a real challenge, but it was something I had to do. I spent ten years there,

and I considered the software we created head and shoulders above our apparel-industry peers in terms of apparel MIS."

But, after his firm merged with a sister company, Gene became disenchanted. "I was the only manager to survive: Every one of my peers was let go," he says. "Not only was I working fifteen hours a day, I couldn't stand the politics. I had to get out."

Making the Break

Gene and a colleague, Jack Wegst, proposed to start their own company, Online Data Systems. They would not create their own software—they would contract with another company, which had already produced an apparel-industry software package for the mainframe, and turn its RPG code into COBOL.

On the strength of one account they picked up at an IBM Bobbin Show, Gene and Jack left to set up their own firm in 1984. "The account paid us $15,000 to $17,000 a month," Gene says. "We had five people, and we were able to get by on that money—barely—because we got a great break on office space. A company that had been established to "incubate" small businesses leased us office space—including telephones, heat, and copying machines—for $3 a square foot annually. The rule was that after three years we'd have to get out to make room for another fledgling company, but that break on office space gave us our start."

Then came the unanticipated pitfalls. "You don't know, when you step off that edge, what to expect," Gene says. "I didn't understand the ramifications of cash flow, of what it meant to put together a business plan, of having responsibility for people. Many times over the next few years I got into trouble financially." Not only did Gene and his group work grueling hours that first year—8 a.m. to midnight—but the company's cash-flow problem was so acute that he couldn't sleep at night.

"But I persevered," Gene says. "My accountant told me along the way, 'You're in bad shape; you should close up,' and I said, 'I don't need that kind of advice,' and kept on going.

"Three years after we started, Online Data Systems had twenty-five employees. In 1986, we rewrote everything for the midrange computer. And around 1991, the company started to turn around."

The Joy of Ownership

Now the business is flourishing And now that Gene has known "the excitement of being your own boss, of making daily decisions for your own company," he declares, "I could never go back to being an IT director again."

"Xperia has a staff of forty-two people, thirty of them development people—programmers, customer support people, trainers. We're a small company, and I try to make it a family," Gene says. "We try to get involved with people on a personal basis—understand what their problems are. Our attitude and atmosphere are different from that in a corporate environment, where there are levels of management. We have a very flat organization, and we have an open-door policy when somebody has a problem.

"We have meetings every three weeks. We bring in lunch, and everyone has an opportunity to air his opinions about the company—what we do well, what we don't do well, what we need to work on. When we make mistakes, they bubble to the surface quickly, because everybody has a problem with them. There's an attitude that we try to bring out in our meetings: If people need help, let's give them all the help they can use. But if they don't want to take the help, let's replace them.

"We pay our people fairly, but we try to reward them periodically—quarterly—with bonuses, based on how well our company does. With that methodology we've managed to keep people at our firm a very long time. If I take new hires out of the equation, our average length of stay for employees is ten years. And remember, our company is only nineteen years old.

"I look for talented people by two methods. I advertise in the paper. I keep it local, within the Allentown area, or go to Philadelphia or New York. I've attracted people from those areas who are looking to get out of the city. If I'm looking for a trainee, there are several local colleges that have a two-year course in COBOL for the iSeries. I have a couple of people here from these schools who are excellent programmers.

"I hired one trainee, and within two and a half years he had gone from $18,000 a year to $50,000. And that's in the Allentown area, where salaries aren't as high as they are in Philadelphia or New York.

In our organization, a super programmer makes $72,000 a year. In Philadelphia that's probably worth $100,000."

Like any entrepreneur, Gene wants to see his company outlive him. And so he recently sold Xperia to his employees. "I offered the employees the opportunity to buy the company," he says, "and they all agreed to participate." Now, he says, his people have an even greater commitment to Xperia's growth and profitability. Under the employee stock option program, the employees have a significant stake in the company; eventually they will own it. "It's a terrific exit strategy—a great way for me to exit the company," he says, "and a great way for the company to continue after I retire."

Is a programmer who likes to sit in front of a computer screen all day likely to make a good entrepreneur? Gene doesn't think so. "If you're going to found your own company, you'd better be gregarious," he says. "You'll spend your day hustling for clients, directing employees, stepping in to resolve conflicts. You'd better not be the retiring type."

$$ The Bottom Line $$

Gene Bonett's advice to new entrepreneurs? Don't do it his way. Don't take the risk of starting your own firm without having an adequate amount of cash in reserve, without understanding cash flow, without knowing how to write a business plan—without, in short, acquiring a realistic idea of the obstacles you might encounter. "Make sure you understand the ramifications of this move into ownership," he says. And, he counsels, pay attention to this truism when you're making your plans: "No matter what contracts you think you're going to sign, they never come through when you think they will."

CHAPTER THIRTY ONE

Inventing Your Own Software

What you enjoy about programming may be the same thing that you would enjoy about entrepreneurship. Using problem-solving skills, creativity, and commitment to create something that initially exists only in your imagination—whether it's a software application, a product, or a company—is one of the great joys in life.

I f you are seriously considering quitting your corporate programming job to develop a software product, here's a glance at the risks and rewards of the inventor's life.

Jason Olim and his twin brother, Matthew, did it the legendary way: When they were 24, they started a business—CDnow—in their parents' basement that went public and became a global brand name.

That was in 1994—not so long ago. That's the great thing about the rapid growth of new technologies: Unknown entrepreneurs, working in modest quarters, without corporate backing, can still come up with a great idea and turn it into computing gold, the way Steve Jobs, Michael Dell, and Bill Gates did at the dawn of the personal-computer age.

You can become a successful inventor at 24, after just a few years in corporate programming, as Jason did. Or you can become an inventor at 60, as I have, after spending a career lifetime as a corporate programmer.

Is it still possible to invent something in your basement? "Absolutely!" Jason declares. "There are phases, life cycles, to new technology. At first there is the core technology, followed by some enabling applications, followed by enabled applications. There is always going to be a new idea. And in any technology's evolution there are always new things to do. Even today, there are new businesses popping up that are entirely next-generation things with the Internet. We will never see invention stop."

Although the idea for CDnow had been brewing slowly for a few years in his subconscious, Jason took a programming job in an electronic mail routing company after graduating from Brown University with a degree in computer science. He was the youngest programmer in a team of eleven very experienced professionals. "I was the only single person in the group," he says. "When they needed someone to go to Hong Kong for a week, or to spend a month in Tokyo, that fell to me. It was great. Filling up my passport was fantastic, the best part of the job." But though he loved his programming job, he left it at age 24. The idea that had been lurking in his subconscious drove him to enter the risky (but heady) world of the software inventor.

The Idea That Wouldn't Let Go

"When I was a freshman in college, somebody lent me Miles Davis's Kind of Blue, which I had never heard before," Jason says. "It really moved me. I thought it was fantastic. I wanted to find more of this wonderful music, so I went to a record store and asked the sales clerk, 'What can you tell me about Miles Davis? I really like Kind of Blue.' And he said, 'Miles Davis is listed under D.'

"This was an accurate answer, but it was clearly not the answer I was looking for. I thought there must be a better way to learn about music, that a record store has a higher calling than just to list albums alphabetically. Over the years, I thought about a variety of things—about clipping album reviews and sticking them to record store shelves, or wearing headphones in the store, and as you picked up a CD you would automatically hear sound samples from the CD. I wanted to find a better way to connect to the music, to appreciate it more deeply and to discover new albums and artists.

"This problem was in my mind for six years. Every time I went to a music store I would think, 'Hmmm, how can this be better?' One day, I had a blinding flash—the answer was an online music store. It occurred to me that I could make a database of all the albums ever created, of all the reviews ever written, of all the biographies of the artists. I could put that on the Internet, people could connect to it, and they could learn about whatever they liked. They could go in and look up Miles Davis's Kind of Blue, learn about the album, look at recommendations, understand what else he has done, and see his career time line. They could really learn about and experience the music. I could support the system by selling the albums. That was the original inspiration, in February of 1994.

"My twin brother, Matthew, actually took over most of the programming, although his background is in astrophysics. I quit my job, he came back from Philadelphia, where he had been pursuing a master's degree in neuroscience, and we both moved back into our parents' house, setting up shop in their basement.

"Matt had no programming background, but he taught himself to program in C. He took out the 1978 Kernighan and Ritchie monograph, the book that originally defined the C programming language, and he read that. The downside of that was that the 1978 version did not include a lot of the improvements, both stylistic and functional, that have occurred in the sixteen years between when the monograph was written and when Matt was reading it. But nonetheless it was a good start for him, and he learned some of the more elegant techniques over time.

"We created a database, buying or licensing information from various books and magazines and other companies that could give us information or the data structures that we needed. So we built a compatible database of all this data that we got from reviews and bios and album titles. We built an interface that people could connect to over the Internet—basically a Web page—and we built a whole processing infrastructure so people could easily select the albums they wanted to buy and get their credit card information, and the CDs would be in a warehouse somewhere and would be picked out and sent to them.

"The time it took from the initial conception to actually selling CDs online was six months. We started a business called CDnow and ran it. In our first month of operation we sold $387 worth of CDs; we had a gross profit of $14. We took the whole gross profit and floated it back into the business and went from there."

Day to Day Life in a Bootstrap Operation

Jason and Matt worked sixteen hours a day, seven days, a week, for the first couple of years—"actually, for most of the seven or eight years that I ran the business," Jason says. "Certainly we worked those hours when ours was a small company, when it was just me and my brother and my buddy from high school whom we were paying $7 an hour to do work for us.

"When the company was small, our responsibilities were a little bit more intertwined. The key issues for our business were to improve the quality of our interface and make it more usable, to improve the quality of our back-end systems, to improve our delivery, and to come up with better cost-management and operational management systems that would also include things like customer service and shipping and mailing systems.

"There was a tremendous operational product. The product was not CDs, but the Web site itself. That's what we worked on. We didn't create CDs, we created a store. Our major effort was to perfect the operational aspect of the store, both in terms of people's experience with the interface itself and our back-end systems to deliver the products that people ordered. And my brother largely took over that because he related to the programming. My responsibility was largely with the marketing and the industry side of the business."

Asked about his perfectionistic bent, Jason says, "Not everyone is like me. I believe that the quest for perfection is sometimes a strength, and sometime it isn't. But it is just the way I am. I believe that the best way to create value in the marketplace is to have a great product. I would always say that a great product sells itself. But that isn't really a true statement. Still, having the resolve to improve the system until it exceeds customers' expectations is the way I work.

"There are other people in the world who are more focused on selling and marketing: They believe that product should be good, but the marketing should be better. That's fine when you're building a business, but it isn't in accord with my values. I think the most important thing is the quality of the product, and so I'm never satisfied. I always want to make sure that I am improving the quality of the product to establish the highest level of playing field as possible. I don't want my competitors to be able to do the same thing I do, and so I have to do it better."

Up and Running

"In our first year of operation—six months of sales in 1994—we did about $60,000 worth of total sales. We advertised in a variety of ways. We'd go online into news groups, and someone would have posted a question saying, 'We're looking for such-and-such an album; does anyone know where we can find it?' And we would respond by saying, 'You can find it at CDnow!'

"Or we would go to the search engines. Back in those days, you could advertise on them for free. If you said to them, 'Hey, we have something that is new and cool—you should put us on your new and cool list,' they'd do it. And so we got Yahoo and Webcrawler and a lot of the old original engines to list us as something new and cool. And, in fact, we got them to list us as something new and cool every week. So we kept trying to do new things that would keep them listing us on their home pages.

"We went into magazine advertising in the fall of 1994, just as we launched the Web site. We bought these third-page black-and-white column ads in Wired magazine. We also hired a public relations firm."

Jason has since sold his business to pursue other interests. He reflects: "What I enjoy about programming is the same thing that I enjoy about entrepreneurship. Using problem-solving skills, creativity, and commitment to create something that initially exists only in your imagination, whether it's a software application, a company, or anything else, is one of the great joys in life. For me, it's the embodiment of the phrase 'Follow your dreams.'"

Indeed.

$$ The Bottom Line $$

It's still possible to turn a good idea into a lucrative software product—and do it on your own, without corporate backing, so that your invention is your intellectual property. You'll need entrepreneurial vision, great coding skills, tenacity, the willingness to work long hours (perhaps for years), along with a passion for your product. You'll also need a nest egg to live on for a few years—or a parent or spouse who's supportive (both financially and emotionally).

CHAPTER THIRTY TWO

Marketing Your Product

For programmers who are thinking of developing software on their own, I offer my initial marketing effort (a debacle) as a cautionary tale. After that, as helpful counterpoint—the advice of someone who did it right.

Like every other software developer on the planet, I am what Jason Olim calls "the visionary"—the person who invented the product, the person who knows what benefits the world can get out of it, the one who can predict how it might be used twenty years down the line. But how does a visionary make people begin to adopt his or her invention?

That's a question I've been yearning to see answered ever since I started working on RTPA, my own project, in 1999. Writing the code was exciting and mentally rewarding. But, though focusing intensely sixteen hours a day, seven days a week, is grueling, the code-writing was the easy part. Marketing was the hard part. The really hard part.

My story—the tale of a "visionary" who couldn't successfully market his product through his and his family's mom-and-pop efforts—is doubtless the story of many basement inventors like me. For programmers who are thinking of developing software on their own, I offer my initial marketing effort (a debacle) as a cautionary tale. After that, as helpful counterpoint—the advice of someone who did it right—I proffer the perspective of Jason Olim, who, with his twin brother, not only created the online music store CDnow (see Chapter 31), but marketed it with great success.

The Mystifying Weakness of the Sensible Approach

RTPA (Real-Time Program Audit) is a software tool that, working with your regular compiler, creates a new program that displays the source statements and variable values of a program. It's the tool I invented to automate the "Harkins Trace," the manual audit described in Chapter 16; RTPA causes a program to create audit files, recording its source statements and variable values while the program executes. When I considered it ready to go into midrange shops everywhere, I went about marketing it in what seemed the sensible way.

I knew that selling was not my strong point. (A talent for pitching a product rarely lurks in pure programmers, who prefer to sit alone in front of a computer screen from morning till night.) But, since I couldn't afford to hire the experts I knew I needed, I took what seemed the logical marketing steps. In my innocence, I assumed they would bring results.

*I rented a $3,000 booth at IBM's semiannual exhibition, COMMON. My wife, Gisela, and I had several banners printed touting RTPA as "The IT Manager's Master Key." I sent press releases out to the editors of the magazines then published for AS/400 (now called iSeries) programmers (*Midrange Computing, NEWS/400, *and other midrange magazines). These editors would be at COMMON. I invited them to a scheduled news conference.*

Then I made a demonstration video for our booth. Because I knew I'd rather stand in the booth and explain my product than buttonhole prospects, I persuaded my articulate and gregarious twin, Peter (he has marketing experience) to be the "plucker." He flourishes on this kind of thing—he'd go into the passing (meaning not-stopping-at-my-booth) crowd, walk up to someone, say, "You program in RPG? Want to double your productivity?" and lead the prospect back to the booth. Then I'd talk my software up and show the video.

I held the news conference for magazine editors. Four editors showed up.

The news conference turned out to be productive. Brian Singleton, editor of Midrange Computing, *wrote an upbeat "hot new products" review, and he also wrote a review online calling RTPA "sort of a trace on steroids." We got similar raves in* NEWS/400 *(now* iSeries NEWS*) and* iSeries *magazines.*

But no sales came directly out of all this. "Not a single sale?" my programming friends and I kept saying to each other. "How could that be?" From our appearance at a second COMMON, we got one sale and a promising prospect. Then we got anther big customer to license RTPA at an apparel industry trade show. It was becoming clear to me that people had to see and try my software product to understand how they could benefit from it. It was just too different from what they were used to.

I bought several of the marketing volumes called Top Computer Executives in the United States *and highlighted 100 big AS/400 shops for marketing calls. Peter made 100 marketing phone calls to the targeted prospects. But he couldn't reach a single one of them live. All of his calls were stopped by an answering machine, and only one of the prospects for whom Pete left his brief pitch called back.*

With the help my sister, Debbie, I made up a packet containing an impressive (we thought) four-color brochure, a demonstration CD, and a series of quotes from enthusiastic users at the three major apparel firms to which I had sold RTPA (through personal contacts). I mailed 400 of them out to executives targeted through the Top Computer Executives *book. Only several of them responded.*

I sought marketing assistance from the SCORE program of the U.S. Small Business Administration (free counseling for entrepreneurs). The marketing expert whom I met had no other suggestions for me. He thought I'd made the right moves for a bootstrapping marketer.

When a $5,000 ad in a magazine aimed at AS/400 programmers yielded not a single sale, I knew I had to find some other way. Fortunately, that's when Jason Olim joined my one-programmer firm.

How his marketing savvy will play out I don't know, for, as I write this, our RTPA marketing campaign has barely begun and we have focused on strengthening the product and simplifying the programmer interface.

Tips from an Inventor with Marketing Savvy

When he was doing the marketing for CDnow, Jason Olim (who was profiled in Chapter 31) says, "I knew I was lucky in that I have a talent for marketing. But that doesn't mean that I am the 'marketing guy' in the way that I am 'product guy.' To get CDnow going, I had to go find people who had skills that I didn't have. So, I went and hired a PR firm; I went and hired an ad person. I got all the advice I could. I held other people accountable to do what I didn't know how to do. I knew what I wanted the result to be, which was more sales, but I didn't know how to do it. TV ads, radio ads, print ads, big giveaways, putting our banners on the sides of buses—I didn't know what to do. I hired other people and said, 'Here's what I want: I want sales of a certain amount of money, and here's how much money I can give you to spend. Can you make it happen?' And the people who could do it were the ones I hired."

That, I've concluded, was my problem with marketing RTPA—lack of the financial wherewithal to hire marketing experts. But Jason disagrees. "Money is by no means the necessary glue," he says. "And even if you can afford to hire a marketing expert, how do you find one? They just don't pop out of the woodwork."

Jason believes that marketing can be done as a mom-and-pop operation. "Some people are innately gifted at crafting their message, so they don't need to hire an expert to write their copy," he says. "But even if you're not innately gifted, there are rules that should lead to marketing success, as long as you follow them."

I asked Jason to look at the copy Debbie and I had created about RTPA and tell us what we'd done wrong. And what did Jason tell us? Our materials did not even communicate what RTPA did—what RTPA was.

Our copy, Jason says, failed to follow the most basic marketing rule: Communicate what it is you're selling. That glossy, four-page brochure we'd created did not paint a clear picture of what RTPA was, and how it worked.

We had come up with a metaphor ("RTPA: The IT Manager's Master Key"). That, Jason says, was too literary; it didn't communicate the tangible benefits of RTPA. "You didn't grab onto the key things that would excite the reader."

What I Could Have Done Better

How could we have been more effective? Jason responded that we should have asked several programmers who were *not* our friends to read the copy and tell us if they understood it. "Show your marketing copy to your friends and they'll tell you it's great," he says. "So don't ask your friends. Go to your target audience—programmers—and say, 'Here's my message. What does this sound like? Do you understand it? How do you feel about it?'

"The inventor should forget what *he* wants the audience to think about the product and ask audience members what *they* think about the product. He should spend time with the potential target buyers, asking them, 'Does this make sense to you? Are you willing to buy this? Will you buy it?' Then he can start writing the marketing materials."

When he was establishing CDnow, Jason's goal was to make his description of the workings of this online store so clear that even his grandmother could understand it. "'Will this make sense to my grandmother?' was my test," he says. Clarity and simplicity of message were vital. "At that time, Web sites advised their visitors to communicate with them by sending an e-mail to ROOT (the UNIX administrator)," Jason says. "We at CDnow were the first to change that word to 'manager.' It was very important to us to communicate that we were a store, an online store, and that you, the visitor, could speak to a customer service person or the manager."

How about the other steps we'd taken, at great effort and formidable (for us) expense—and that had yielded so few sales?

Renting the booth at COMMON and holding the news conferences were good moves, Jason acknowledges. "Getting press coverage is a very powerful way of communicating," he says. "It's good as part of your marketing program, but it won't create sales by itself. Contrary to inventors' expectations, a favorable editorial mention in a magazine isn't going to establish your company."

As for the magazine ad that yielded nothing, that didn't surprise Jason either. "An ad isn't going to create a tornado of interest in your product. In any given magazine, you'll see hundreds of thousands of marketing dollars' worth of ads touting products, to create a little bit of awareness that the product is out there. You use an ad in combination with all your other marketing tactics.

"What is the gap between an ad and a sale? Is the customer being told to do something NOW in that ad—dial this number, clip this coupon? The ad needs to challenge the reader to take some physical action right now."

As for the lack of response to our 100 marketing calls and 400 marketing letters, "in a market this small," Jason says, "it's not unreasonable not to get a nibble." Direct marketers know that the response rate is very low. What we had definitely done wrong was to make only one phone call, send only one letter, to each prospect. "What," Jason said incredulously, "you didn't call back two or three times? You never approach a prospect just once.

"Sure, telemarketing is painful," he says. There's a tremendous amount of rejection. But if you set out to contact a customer, you've got to contact him more than once. There are books about the gambits you need to use to get through to people live and set up appointments," he says.

"Just because your product is good doesn't mean that you deserve to be able to sell it—that your customer is wrong if he doesn't buy it. It's up to you to make him want to buy it. Until your customer uses your product, you have work to do."

$$ The Bottom Line $$

Your idea for an invention may be brilliant. But does the market know about it and want it? How will you know? Can you afford to take a flyer—quit your corporate programming job, max out your credit cards, put a second mortgage on the house, borrow from your pension fund—to find out? Be warned that if you do make the jump, your experience as an independent software developer may renew your appreciation for the rewards of life as a highly paid—and regularly paid—corporate programmer. On the other hand, you may be in for the adventure of a lifetime.